THE GOVERNOR'S STORY

MERLE COLLINS

THE GOVERNOR'S STORY

THE AUTHORIZED BIOGRAPHY
OF DAME HILDA BYNOE

PEEPAL TREE

First published in Great Britain in 2013
Peepal Tree Press Ltd
17 King's Avenue
Leeds LS6 1QS
England

ISBN13: 9781845232245

Supported using public funding by
ARTS COUNCIL
ENGLAND

ACKNOWLEDGEMENTS

This book began as an idea presented by Dame Hilda Bynoe and her family. I accepted, with enthusiasm, the task of research and writing. It could not have been completed without the cooperation of Dame Hilda and her sons, Roland and Michael (Mickey). Early in the process, Mickey answered some key questions and helped me understand the role of the family in Dame Hilda's responses to events. Roland was always available to respond to emails, follow up on questions, arrange Skype interviews when necessary, and to ensure transportation from the airport or other location to Dame Hilda's home. I thank Roland's daughter and Dame Hilda's granddaughter, Olukemi (Kemi) for being available to set up Skype interviews. I recognise great granddaughter Anaia's role in keeping Dame Hilda's eyes on the possibilities of the future.

I acknowledge the assistance of the St George's University, which made it possible for me to spend one summer dedicating my time exclusively to writing and research for this work. Similarly, one semester's sabbatical from the University of Maryland afforded me the valuable gift of time for research and writing.

A work like this benefits from the conversation and thoughtful interventions of many. My thanks to Mr Caldwell Taylor, Grenada's Ambassador to the United Nations during the 1979-83 period, and an excellent researcher of world history and Caribbean life and letters. Caldwell guided me to valuable sources and was always ready to respond to questions and offer suggestions. Dr Dorith Grant-Wisdom, Lecturer in the Honors Program, University of Maryland, was ready with a keen eye for detail and useful advice. Ms Gloria Payne-Banfield, with a deep interest in and knowledge of local and family history, generously responded to questions and offered clarification about puzzling details. Dr Antonia MacDonald Smythe, St George's University, Grenada, gave important assistance from the early days of the development of this project. Toward the end of the project, when I continued to have questions about some of the family stories surrounding the early life of Ma Harriet (Mayet), Dame Hilda Bynoe's maternal ancestor, my questions resulted in the coming together of various members of the family, descendants of Mayet and her children. They contacted each other by email, and copied me in on the correspondence, explaining ancestral links between the McGilchrists, Preudhommes, Archers and various other families – in Grenada and locations throughout the world – connected with Dame Hilda Bynoe's maternal family line.

In less tangible, but equally appreciated ways, my family and friends contributed by their support to the existence of this work. I value every contribution.

CONTENTS

FOREWORD

In *Biographer and Subject: A Tale of Two Narratives,* Allen Hibbard suggests a dialectical relationship between two stories in the crafting of a biography: "The enterprise of writing biography necessarily involves two distinct, yet related narrative strands: the story of the subject and the story of the biographer coming to know, structure, and recreate the life of the subject." Hibbard notes that, "biography itself, as a genre, usually effaces or even erases the stories of biographers' sleuthing and journeys in the interest of creating a clear, coherent, linear narrative of the subject's life."[1] Hibbard seems particularly interested in the biographies that do not seek to disguise the biographer's role, but to acknowledge its effect on the shaping of the narrative. As I will outline below, Hibbard's focus is particularly pertinent to my own history in coming to this biography.

Raising a rather different but connected issue, the American historian Barbara Tuchman writes, "…insofar as I have used biography in my work, it has been less for the sake of the individual subject than as a vehicle for exhibiting an age."[2] From the start of my involvement in this project, the life story of Dame Hilda Bynoe seemed an excellent vehicle for exploring the age and the region that shaped her, but this broader conception of the biographical subject meant that I had to consider my role even more carefully.

This was not least because, throughout the writing of this biography, Dame Hilda had very clear perceptions about the story she wanted to tell. After her responses to the first draft, I began to wonder whether my role was largely that of an amanuensis, and I began to think about the story of the abolitionist biographer Susanna Strickland's role in the writing of *The History of Mary Prince* in 1831. Was Strickland simply the one who held the pen or did she have a more significant editorial role? Historians have questioned how far

Strickland shaped Mary Prince's orally narrated story into something
that presented an unambiguous polemic for abolition, even if this
meant casting Prince in a role of victimhood that denied her a degree
of agency.[3]

My own connection with this biography began, I suppose, in
1968, when my high school, St Joseph's Convent, St George's,
Grenada, was, like the rest of the country, abuzz with the news that
Dr Hilda Gibbs Bynoe, Grenadian resident in neighbouring Trinidad, was to be Grenada's new Governor, replacing the British
national Sir Ian Turbott, who was then in office. The complication
was that the person who suggested Dr Bynoe for appointment to
office was Grenada's Premier during the last days of the British
colonial system, a flamboyant and controversial political figure.
Exciting, confusing, inspiring, disturbing, the news of Dr Bynoe's
prospective appointment seemed to my high school classmates and
me to have all the elements of good drama. It disturbed because
Premier Eric Gairy and my generation of youth were engaged in
bitter conflict, but the appointment of a woman Governor, and one
of our own, also seemed to signal change and say something
posititive about the role of women in the shaping of postcolonial
Caribbean societies. This aspect of the announcement loomed
large in our imaginations.

Dr Bynoe took office as Governor of Grenada on June 8th, the
same day that the assassinated Senator Robert Kennedy was laid to
rest at Arlington National Cemetery in the USA. Two months
earlier, Martin Luther King had also been slain. Perhaps it is
understandable that, given the tenor of the times, my generation of
students at the St Joseph's Convent High School, St George's,
Grenada, would be, in our teenage certainties, admiring but distant,
impressed yet offhand.

One of the surprise finds of my research was an article in a local
Grenada newspaper, *The Torchlight*, reporting that Grenada's new
Governor visited St Joseph's Convent, and "was welcomed to the
school by sixth form student, Miss Merle Collins".[4] This was a time
of tremendous political upheaval in the island but I have no memory
of delivering the welcome. I contacted a 1968 classmate to ask if she
remembered details relating to Dr Bynoe's visit. She did not, though
she could also remember that the visit took place and could recall the
local and international political tensions of the period. As far as I

know, that early connection has no role in my responding enthusi-
astically when asked to write Dame Hilda's biography. Perhaps I was
simply as fascinated by the story of Dr Bynoe then as I am now. But
there are other perspectives to consider in this recounting.

In the years after 1968, I had been a young woman actively
involved in the popular agitation of the period. I had written about
that period and its aftermath in my novel, *Angel* (1987/2010).[5] I had
undoubted views on the politics of the period. How far did I want to
edit and analyse Dame Hilda's story? Whatever the answer to this, I
came to realise that, as Hibbard indicates, there remain questions of
choice and interpretation. Indeed, there are two stories, and unless
the decision is taken to render them as two separate accounts – one
possibly a ghosted autobiography, the other in interview format with
roles clearly demarcated – there has to be negotiation to produce what
Hibbard refers to as a coherent, linear narrative. What appears here
is the story that negotiation has produced, a story which is, in my
estimation, an important one because it makes us think creatively
about postcolonial becoming.

What became clear was that Dame Hilda's story could not be told
without reference to its wider, indeed worldwide historical context.
1968, the year in which Dr Hilda Bynoe was appointed governor,
was also, coincidentally, the year I graduated from high school. It was
the year in which political unrest in Grenada was a microcosm of the
socio-political upheavals arising throughout the world.

The writer Mark Kurlansky describes 1968 as "unique" because
"people were rebelling over disparate issues and had in common only
that desire to rebel, ideas about how to do it, a sense of alienation from
the established order, and a profound distaste for authoritarianism in
any form."[6] Kurlansky documents such elements of the challenge to
the established order as the civil rights struggle in the USA, opposition to the Vietnam war, student unrest in Europe and the rise of
Palestinian demands for national self-determination. He explains
the global situation in this way:

> Four historic factors merged to create 1968: the example of the civil
> rights movement, which at the time was so new and original, a generation
> that felt so different and so alienated that it rejected all forms of authority,
> a war that was hated so universally around the world that it provided
> a cause for all the rebels seeking one; and all of this occurring at the
> moment that television was coming of age but was still new enough

not to have yet become controlled, distilled, and packaged the way
that it is today. In 1968 the phenomenon of a same-day broadcast
from another part of the world was in itself a gripping new technological
wonder.[7]

Kurlansky also names 1968 as "an important year for women,
not because of skirt lengths but because of events such as Muriel
Siebert announcing on January 1 that she had become the first
woman to own a seat on the New York Stock Exchange in its
175-year history."[8]

He writes, too, in the book, *1968: The world Transformed*, that: "the
events of 1968 happened within national contexts yet took place
across the globe – from Berkeley to Berlin, Bangkok to Buenos Aires,
Cairo to Cape Town, Paris to Tokyo. In addition, many contemporaries – particularly students and intellectuals – believed that their
actions were linked to a global revolt against capitalism, imperialism
and colonialism that spanned the First, Second and Third Worlds."[9]
Throughout the world, there was student protest against the war in
Vietnam and these protests sometimes became linked with local
agitation against governments considered too conservative and too
willing to defend the status quo. In West Germany, student activists
confronted the conservative media and the German government. In
France in May 1968, there were violent confrontations between
police and students, with students standing their ground and fighting
back and a surge of worker occupations of factories. It was possible to
believe in that year that capitalism and neo-imperialism were totter-
ing.

The Caribbean was caught up in this ferment. There had been
enough time following independence in Jamaica and Trinidad (in
1962), for youth, radical intellectuals and workers to see a new elite
securing power but showing reluctance to decolonise inherited
social, economic and cultural structures.

In October 1968, prominent Guyanese historian Walter Rodney,
lecturer and activist at the Mona, Jamaica campus of the University
of the West Indies, was barred from Jamaica by the government of
Prime Minister Hugh Shearer. In Trinidad, an array of radical groups
from Black cultural nationalist NJAC (National Joint Action Committee), to Dr Lloyd Best's[10] Tapia House Movement were developing critiques of and popular opposition to the politics of the towering
and increasingly authoritarian figure of Prime Minister Dr Eric

Williams that eventually manifested in the Black Power Uprising of 1970. In Grenada, there were demonstrations against the government of Premier Eric Matthew Gairy, who, although he disdainfully advised "Black Power" advocates that he had been the country's first proponent of "Black Power",[11] was considered by many among the new generation of youth to be repressive and dictatorial. For students from smaller islands study in Jamaica in particular was a radicalising experience, and an affirmation that individual island struggles were part of a greater whole.

For young people and students in the Caribbean there was also the example of Cuba. In 1968, for the ninth anniversary of its revolution, Cuba erected "a sixty-foot high mural of the thirty-eight-year-old Argentine Ernesto "Che" Guevara, who had been killed in Bolivia two months earlier while carrying out what Cuba considered his revolutionary duties in the struggles of neighbouring countries.[12] 1968 was a year in which young people, exposed to ideas of revolution and change, willed much for their own countries.

For all Caribbean countries, then, this was a transitional period. Officially, these were the last days of colonial rule. Some of the islands had already achieved Independence – Jamaica and Trinidad & Tobago in 1962, and Barbados and Guyana in 1966 – and other countries of the Caribbean were also moving towards acquiring legal status as Independent states. The new guard, therefore, was being assembled for a leadership role but the indicators of transition were unsettling.

So what I set out to do was write an individual story, a family story, an island story but to see these elements in the context of world change. The word was not yet in vogue in 1968, but this narrative, one of whose subtexts is the theme of migration – both out of and within the Caribbean – inevitably brings to mind the term "globalization". As Thomas Klak notes, "Some globalization writers argue that the world is 'shrinking'; this socially and spatially uneven trend is nothing new to Caribbean people".[13] Klak notes that the term globalization is sometimes reduced by scholars to a discussion about migration – and certainly Dr Bynoe's story presents an experience relating to what Klak refers to as this "compression of the world's peoples, places, and nation-states, as well as a blurring of their territorial boundaries"[14] – but beyond the story of migration in the creation and development of a Caribbean diaspora, perhaps the largest context for this narrative is the fact that Caribbean people have been experiencing the political,cultural and economic consequences of globalization for over four hundred years.

In the end, though, this is a story of a significant individual, and my narrative asks: Who was she, this young Grenadian woman who had returned from the neighbouring island, Trinidad, to accept the top ceremonial post in a small British Commonwealth nation during the last years of its existence as a colony of Britain? This biography aims to answer that question and to consider the complex interweaving of the personal and the more broadly political in the story of Dame Hilda Bynoe.

Endnotes

1. Alan Hibbard, "Biographer and Subject: A Tale of Two Narratives", *South Central Review,* Johns Hopkins University Press,Volume 23, Number 3, (Fall 2006), pp. 19-36.
2. Barbara Tuchman, "Biography as a Prism of History", quoted in Stephen B. Oates, *Biography as High Adventure: Life writers speak on their art* (The University of Massachusetts Press, 1986), p. 93
3. See the introduction of Moira Ferguson to *The History of Mary Prince* (Michigan: University of Michigan Press, 1997).
4. *The Torchlight*. St George's, Grenada: June 10, 1968.
5. My novel, *Angel*, first published by the Women's Press in 1987, and reissued in a revised edition by Peepal Tree Press in 2010, is a fictional exploration of the years from the rise of Gairy to the implosion of the PRG (Provisional Revolutionary Government) and the American invasion.
6. Mark Kurlansky, *1968: The Year That Rocked The World* (New York: Random House, 2004), p. xvii.
7. Mark Kurlansky, op.cit,, p. xviii.
8. Kurlansky, p. 20.
9. See *1968: The World Transformed*, Ed. Carole Fink, Philipp Gassert and Detlef Junker (Cambridge: Cambridge University Press, 1998), p. 1.

10. See Norman Girvan, "Lloyd Best: A Great Conceptualiser",
Trinidad & Tobago Review, Port-of-Spain. November, 2005. http:/
/www.normangirvan.info/lloyd-best-a-great-conceptualiser/
and see Gordon Rohlehr, "Remembering Lloyd Best", *Caribbean
Review of Books,* March 23, 2007.http://www.meppublishers.com/
online/crb/issues/index.php?pid=1073.
11. Radio Broadcast by Sir Eric Gairy, Premier of Grenada, delivered
on Sunday 3rd and Monday 4th May, 1970.
12. Kurlansky, p. 20.
13. Thomas Klak, *Globalization and Neoliberalism: the Caribbean
context* (Lanham: Rowman & Littlefield, 1998), p. 5
14. Thomas Klak, *Globalization and Neoliberalism: The Caribbean
Context,* pp. 5-13. Klak offers a fascinating discussion of
globalization as it affects the Caribbean, moving from the global
village and migration aspects of the term to a consideration
of Caribbean political economy in a global context, when the
term seems less celebratory of Caribbean "global" experience.
He observes, "Contrary to the universalistic notion of a 'global
village' – in which the world is in various ways coming together,
synthesizing, and balancing out, the Caribbean may be better
depicted as a region that is increasingly irrelevant in economic
and geopolitical terms. At one level, this is an ironic statement.
Indeed, Caribbean *people* are more internationally integrated
than ever before, thanks to the unprecedented scale of the
Caribbean diaspora in North Atlantic countries and the associated
remittances. But the massive scale of contemporary emigration
and remittances is the result of growing marginalization and
pessimism about the economic prospects back home" (p. 13).

CHAPTER ONE
TOWARDS AN UNDERSTANDING OF THE PERIOD
AND THE INDIVIDUAL

On June 8, 1968, Dr Hilda Louisa Bynoe, née Gibbs, a medical doctor resident in Trinidad, was formally appointed to the office of Governor of the Caribbean state of Grenada.[1] This was the highest office in the country, and, until that date, only white male British Colonial Office appointees had held the post. The period marked the beginning of the end of colonial rule as, under the Associated Statehood Act of 1967, Grenada became an "Associated State" of Britain, with control over its internal affairs – Britain retaining responsibility for "any matter which in the opinion of the Government of the United Kingdom relates to defence and external affairs".[2] In 1969, following her appointment as Governor, the Queen bestowed on Dr Bynoe the title Dame Commander of the British Empire,[3] the two actions signifying both colonial patronage *and* colonial disentanglement, making Dame Hilda an overt symbol of the contradictions of postcolonial identity. With her appointment, Dame Hilda inherited the pomp, ceremony and respect due to an office traditionally occupied by a male white representative of the British Crown. As a different sort of representative, female and local-born, time was yet to show how Governor Bynoe would interpret the demands of her office.

With an area of 344 square kilometres or 133 square miles, the State of Grenada comprises the islands Grenada, the largest at 120 square miles, Carriacou and Petite Martinique. Originally inhabited by Amerindian peoples and, from the 15th century, claimed, occupied and colonised by various European countries, Grenada shares with other islands in the Caribbean, as well as with Guyana in South America and Belize in Central America, a history of colonisation by Britain and therefore some commonalities of language, culture and historical antecedents.

The demographics of Grenada and neighbouring Caribbean countries followed European demands for labour to cultivate sugar cane

Map of Grenada

fields and exploit other natural resources. The enslaved population in Grenada rose from 525 in 1700 (a period of French colonial control)[4] to 23,536 in 1833, the year in which the British parliament, pressurised by the continuous struggles of enslaved Africans in the Caribbean and urged by Europe's awakening conscience, and lessening opposition from the West India interests in the face of decreasing profits, passed an Act for the Abolition of slavery.[5]

As in most neighbouring Caribbean countries, the official end of chattel slavery in Grenada came with Emancipation in August 1838. In the immediate post-Emancipation period, many estates, unable to be competitive, went out of business, and were eventually abandoned. Those who were once enslaved established smallholdings around former estates, laying the foundation for the villages and smallholdings that exist today. Around the middle of the nineteenth century, many of the estates that continued to exist moved from sugar to cocoa and nutmeg production. Meantime, in Carriacou, part of the tri-island state, sugar production was replaced by the production of corn and pigeon peas. In the immediate post-emancipation period, as some Grenadian planters continued to try to keep costs low and make estates viable, there was an attempt to supplement the labour pool with indentured Africans and Indians. Generally, the once enslaved Africans wanted their own plots of land. One observer offered the opinion that "the planter must be well aware that every Negro to whom he is paying wages has at heart a longing and determination sooner or later to possess a piece of land of his own, or at all events to hire and occupy one, which he can cultivate in his own way, and at his own convenience, and not at his employer's dictation. The object of the planter and the labourer are therefore directly opposed one to the other."[6] The historian Alvin Thompson notes that, in the post-Emancipation period, while sugar remained the dominant crop in some countries – Cuba, Guyana, Suriname, Trinidad – in others like Grenada, St Vincent, Haiti, Jamaica, it suffered a drastic decline.[7] Small farming, which had started in Grenada even pre-emancipation, developed rapidly in the post-emancipation period. Grenada's terrain was hilly and workers had discovered early that tree crops were successful. According to Pugh and Momsen, "this fact shaped the evolution of agriculture and land tenure after Emancipation on Grenada in a unique way in the region."[8] Several other researchers refer to the development of smallholdings in Grenada and opportunities for those once enslaved to acquire land.[9] Noting that some proprietors developed their failing estates into smaller plots and sold them to the peasantry, one writer comments also on the hardships of the period: "Generally, the post-emancipation century passed by painfully for the Grenadian colony. The vagaries of the world market meant that Grenada's material fortunes ebbed and flowed."[10]

As we try to understand the relationship between such social formations in Grenadian society, and the associated cultural frameworks and social attitudes that had developed by the time of Dr Bynoe's formative years, it is worth considering how the sociologist M.G. Smith characterised the Grenadian society that emerged in the 1950s and 60s. Though from contemporary perspectives M.G. Smith's terminology is sometimes troubling (one notes, for example, the belittling and reductive terms used to characterise traditional African religions), he offers some useful insights. Eschewing broad divisions into classes, Smith settled on the terms "folk" and "elite" to divide the society into broad, diametrically opposed groups. Those he described as "folk" were, generally speaking, "poor in property, resources and skills", and largely of the African and Indian groups who were descended from slaves and indentured servants. His analysis suggests that the folk would adhere to, or have broad sympathies with, aspects of traditional Africa present in the society like the shango (traditional Yoruba religion) and saracca. On the other side were the planting class and those descended from them, whom Smith described as "elites". Smith characterised these groups in the early 1950s as "two sharply different populations whose association traditionally presumed subordination of the majority to the regulating institutions and power of the few."[11] In the society that he saw emerging, there were, Smith assessed, "racial and cultural hybrids" who occupied "the interval between the extremes".[12] From the end of emancipation to the beginning of the 1950s, Smith argued, there was an accommodation between these two opposed groups, with the "folk" having no political representation. In the 1950s, such representation began to emerge and the uneasy consensus that had existed between these opposing groups since emancipation was over. Generally, according to Smith, "elite" and "folk" were sharply distinguished by their behaviour, ideas, speech, associations, appearance, colour, housing, occupation, status, access to resources, and in other ways."[13] For all the deficiences of Smith's analysis (his neglect of the dynamics of class formation, and a more complicated relationship between culture and class than he appears to allow) his work does point to features that had an impact on the organisation of classes in the society, on the working class perceptions of itself, on the composition and organisation of the peasantry and on the self-identification of the middle classes. This analysis has a bearing on the attitudes towards and perceptions of the family groups that helped shape Dame Hilda Bynoe's sensibilities. She was proud of her African ancestry and origins among the working people, and her story suggests early association with and continuing sympathy for those described by Smith as the "folk". In an essay examining hegemonic and counter-hegemonic tendencies in the Grenada Revolution of 1979-1983, Gail Pool draws attention to what she terms the "creative base of Grenadian culture" and notes, importantly, that Antonio Gramsci viewed culture as an important part of the formation of ideologies.[14] This perspective might help explain how the Governor's politics were influenced by her interest in ideals and attitudes common among the "folk". One might say that those described by Smith as the folk progressively found a place in the various classes emerging during the post-emancipation period, accommodating themselves to ideas and attitudes extant among the elite whilst also retaining positive attitudes to folk culture. Consonant with this, and reflecting changes in factors such as economic status, levels of education and political influence within the society, there emerged notions such as lower middle class, middle class and other designations such as the "aspiring" working class. These suggest both a more dynamic and complex pattern than M.G. Smith's elite/folk dichotomy and the emergence of challenges to and changes in the nature of the elite. Less reductive than M.G. Smith in their analysis of the changing times during the hundred years after Emancipation, Kaufman et al allow for "a rising black and mixed middle class" in Grenada during the first years of the twentieth century. This group, they noted, "began to challenge both the Crown and the planter class", and included "labor intellectuals" such as T.A. Marryshow.[15] After Marryshow in Grenada came a politician more closely aligned with the folk who worked on the estates, and so more effectively poised to break the uneasy elite/folk consensus.

The post-war period of the late 1940s and 1950s was, for the British Caribbean, a period of increasing localised decision-making and the emergence of trade unions, mass political parties and political leaders. The progress of political events during this period was influenced by political developments in Britain, where the Labour Government of 1945-51, with a policy shaped by Fabian socialism, and working to develop these ideas within the contradictory framework of colonial imperial policy, gave a degree of support to the idea of increased devolution of power to the colonies.[16]

In some ways, Grenada's modern story of post-war decolonisation, and the journey of Dame Hilda Louisa Bynoe towards the governorship, has its genesis in part in the ascendency of a local-born politician and union leader, Eric Matthew Gairy, who was later to recommend to the British Crown Dr Bynoe's appointment. Dame Hilda's rise also has its genesis in the changing social relations of gender in the twentieth century Caribbean and in particular Caribbean women's perception of their role in politics and development. Feminist scholar Eudine Barriteau includes the Caribbean in her contention that "the philosophical contradictions of liberal ideologies predispose states to institute unjust gender systems."[17] Assessing the changes that took place during the twentieth century, Barriteau concludes that "through a combination of indigenous and external pressures, the evolving Caribbean state has altered women's unequal access to its resources. It has removed, amended or reformed the legal inferiority or dependency assigned to women in constitutions and laws." Like other liberal feminists, Dr Bynoe participated in this challenge to laws that enshrined a notion of women's inferiority. Gloria Payne-Banfield, who was a prominent civil servant in Grenada for a number of years, states that, "Dame Hilda's appointment provided Grenadian and Caribbean women with inspiration, encouragement and hope in those critical years prior to the 1975 United Nations International Women's Conference (Mexico), when the clamour for the recognition of equal rights for women was, at last, receiving some attention throughout the international community".[18]

In a more controversial way, Eric Gairy may also be said to have had some impact on the twentieth century status of women. In fact, as we consider Hilda Bynoe within the age that produced her, it is also important to trace Eric Gairy's journey towards his decision to appoint a woman governor.

In July 1950, recently returned from Aruba, where he had been a migrant worker, Eric Gairy, then twenty-nine, registered a workers' organisation, the Manual and Mental Workers' Union. Gairy was then a vocal representative of Grenadian youth, the children of the working people determined to struggle against perceived injustices meted out to their own and their parents' generation of workers. By 1 August, 1950, Eric Gairy's new party, the Grenada People's Party, held its first meeting in celebration of Emancipation Day, the day in 1838 when Africans in the West Indies secured the legal termination of their enslavement.[19] In this recognition of the history of his country's working peoples, Eric Gairy was well ahead of his time, since events celebrating Emancipation Day gained wider currency in Grenada only during the first few years of the twenty-first century. Eric Gairy, with a working-class folk sensibility, and having established both union and party, set about organising among and agitating on behalf of estate workers.

In the year following Gairy's organisation of both the union and the political party, on 15 June 1951, the Grenada (Legislative Council) Order in Council, 1951, came into operation. This provided, for the first time, for elections under universal adult suffrage and the removal of property and income qualifications previously required of candidates for election.[20] Adult suffrage transformed Grenadian politics, as it was transforming politics in neighbouring Caribbean countries. After a series of union victories for the working people, though with a developing reputation as more of an individualistic union and political boss than as a party political organiser, Gairy had a significant victory in the 1951 elections. A. W. Singham's important book, *The Hero and the Crowd in a Colonial Polity* (1968), is a pertinent study of Gairy as a populist, crowd-pleasing but increasingly authoritarian figure. He was to continue to be the major political leader in Grenada for the next twenty-eight years. For an understanding of Eric Gairy's influence in Grenadian politics during these years, one needs to consider the polarisation between planters and peasantry, the underlying differences in culture between those described by Smith as "folk" and "elite", and the attempt to maintain a consensus, by the dominant religious, educational and official administrative institutions, that this was the "natural" order of society. But these groups did not have any intrinsic sympathy for each other and Gairy's emergence as someone keen to represent workers and peasantry was generally welcomed by a group which until then had no political representation. A woman in her nineties, who did not identify herself as a supporter of Gairy, confirmed the truth of an idea I used in my novel, *Angel*.[21] Explaining the practice of planters who wanted their estates worked, planted in tree crops like cocoa at little cost, she said, "these people, they give you the land and tell you it is yours to work, and just when it is time for you to reap, they tell you they will take it back, and they give you another piece". She paused and added, "they leave the door wide open". Wide open, I understood, for the advent of a politician like Eric Gairy. The suggestion here is that while increasingly Gairy may have revealed himself as an authoritarian figure, the working people's sense of an oppressive plantocracy made them welcome someone who presented himself as working in their interests, who knew the workings of the estate system and was not intimidated by the bosses. In a highly polarised society, with a "folk" group newly enfranchised (identified by M.G. Smith in 1953 as comprising approximately 94% of the population),[22] any champion of the peasantry would be a popular political figure.

Eric Gairy was well acquainted with the narratives of the working people on whose behalf he had established union and political organisations, and *narrative*, personal or otherwise, is important to an understanding of events. When Eric Gairy was a child, living with his parents, Douglas Gairy and Theresa Gairy, in the environs of Dun-fermline and Mt Horne estates in rural St Andrew's, his father worked as a driver on the Mt Horne estate. A plantation post inherited from the days of enslavement, the driver was responsible for ensuring that the estate workers did their work – his job was to "drive" them. Needed constantly to be present on the estate, Eric Gairy's father was required to live in the estate house allocated to the "driver", and he was seldom at home with his family. Eric, as a boy, was always moving between his parents, acting as a messenger linking the male and female authority figures in his life. He became very familiar with estate conditions, with the workers' expressed needs and with the attitudes of those who owned and/or managed the estates. He heard people of his parents' age and older being referred to as "boy" and "girl". He learnt at firsthand lessons about the place of race and class in a colonial plantation society; about the urban/rural divide; the role of women in the plantation economy – for instance in the house of the estate owner he learnt that there was an effective apartheid in the economic organisation of Grenadian society. He was sometimes on the estate tennis courts (available only to whites), acting as a ball boy, chasing tennis balls as the white estate owners and managers enjoyed their sport. These were all lessons that were important to him as he sought, in his own way, to reform the society of which he became the leader, and redress some of the grievances and disadvantages of working men and women. Towards the end of the 1960s, Gairy was careful to appoint women to his cabinet. These appointments suggest that, whatever may have been other limitations in the exercise of his authority, and despite the fact that he was developing a reputation as a womaniser (see Chapter 5 for Dr Bynoe's reference to this) Gairy was at least aware of the need for change. Grenadian cultural historian Caldwell Taylor also notes that when he began his 1967 term of office, Chief Minister Gairy not only promoted women to higher ranks within his government, but also appointed women to positions of authority in public works positions – "road work", as it was popularly known, appointing women as road drivers. According to Taylor, a road worker named Andolina, of Grenville, St Andrew's, was the first such promotion.[23] This perception is supported by social historian Nicole Phillip who also notes the "increase seen in the number of women appointed in the government."[24] All of this suggests that by 1968, Premier Gairy's receptivity to the idea of having a woman as Governor of the emerging state was not an isolated inclination.

Hilda Louisa Gibbs, second daughter of T. Joseph Gibbs and his wife Louisa Gibbs, née La Touche, was born on November 18, 1921, in Crochu, St Andrew's, on the north-eastern side of the island. She was younger than her sister Josephine by twelve years. Hilda's father told her many stories about his earlier life. On Sundays, he rode to church in his horse and trap, as did another person in the area, Sir Joseph De La Mothe. At the church, there was a shaded tree, and by some stroke of fortune, Sir Joseph would always be in the shade of the tree and Hilda's father would have to park his horse and trap in the sun. One day, divining fortune's hand, Joseph Gibbs went early to church, and, finding the shady tree unoccupied, he put his horse in that coveted spot. The priest asked Joseph to remove his horse. He refused. And so was born a story that T. Joseph Gibbs recounted to his children, advising them that they should stand up against what seemed unfair, regardless of who was meting out the treatment.

This is one of the classical stories about the shaping of the sensibility of what might be termed a Caribbean middle class, aware of the privileges given to white officials and the titled elite who held sway in the colonies, and determined not to be subservient. When told this story, I did not have to wonder (as I might have had to do if told a similar story set in the post-independence period) if Sir Joseph was white and British. My assumption was indeed correct.

Among those who won a seat under the party banner of the Grenada People's Party in 1951 was Thomas Joseph Gibbs, popularly known as Uncle Joe, a candidate for the parish of St David's.

In an analysis of the social forces that produced Dr Eric Williams, Prime Minister of neighbouring Trinidad & Tobago from 1955 to 1981, Gordon Rohlehr, one of the region's most perceptive literary and cultural critics, writes:

> The most intimate portrait that we have of the society that produced Williams is C.L.R. James' warm depiction in *Beyond a Boundary* of the aspiring and respectable puritanical black lower-middle or upper-lower class of the 1920s, whose avenue towards self-betterment was education. As James portrays it, this class was tough, stoical, rigidly moral and powerfully focused in its drive towards excellence. It would produce both stiffly starched colonials and, in a younger generation, either latent black nationalists or the variety of socialist ideologues who began to appear between the 1930s and 1940s and whose ideas and energies would be absorbed in the nationalist movement that Williams was to lead in the mid-1950s.[25]

Hilda Bynoe was not in the mould of Williams, but her life and expressed views suggest that she was a mixture of some of the qualities suggested by Rohlehr. Bynoe was powerfully focused in the drive towards excellence. She was nationalist, assertive about her African heritage, and proud of the mixed Caribbean (Carib, African and European) history that produced her.[26]

The lesson imparted by T. Joseph Gibbs' story – and many others of a similar nature that the girls had from their parents – was deeply imbibed. Much later, Hilda Gibbs, training as a medical doctor in England, would write poems that spoke of the pride and social sensibility inherited from her parents:

> The woman told the story
> About the hurt, anger
> Rage of the people.
>
> She ought to know

She is one of those people
One of those self-same people.[27]

The sense of being "one of those self-same people" was later to
be a part of Dame Hilda's modus operandi in her role as Governor,
and it conditioned her responses to many situations she was to
encounter.

Among other influences for the young Hilda was the Grenadian
politician Theophilus Albert Marryshow, who, by Dr Bynoe's own
account, played an important role in her early politicisation.
Marryshow, popularly known as T.A., ardently supported the regional movement towards a federation of the West Indies. As a
federalist, Marryshow was interested not only in the development of
Grenada, but also in a union of those countries which had more in
common in socio-political and economic terms, and their shared
experience of British colonialism, than any objective differences to
divide them. The motto of *The West Indian*, the newspaper Marryshow
founded, was "The West Indies must be West Indian."[28] Speaking of
Marryshow's impact on her life, Dr Bynoe mentions being told about
the early post World War One days, when Marryshow began speaking about the importance of West Indian unity. She knew, too, how
Marryshow had agitated against the then Colonial Secretary Blood.[29]
"He got the people to march and say that Blood must go." Marryshow's
example is mentioned by other people who came to be influential in
world politics. Wilfred Little, the brother of Malcolm X, wrote about
the influence of Marryshow's newspaper, *The West Indian,* in his own
family. According to Wilfred Little, his mother, who was from
Grenada, used to read passages from this newspaper aloud to her
children. Marryshow was "somebody she boasted about all the
time".[30] Marryshow was clearly important in the shaping of ideas
among that generation of Grenadian people, and, indeed, had
significance in the shaping of ideas in the Caribbean and African
diaspora.

Caldwell Taylor notes that the Marryshow of Hilda Gibbs's
childhood was a radical figure, openly and effectively challenging the
colonial administration so that in time it made the kind of constitutional concessions that benefited Eric Gairy. Taylor notes that in
1917, Marryshow founded the Representative Government Association (RGA) to agitate for a new and participative constitutional

dispensation for the Grenadian people.[31] When, in 1925, Grenada was granted a New Constitution, representing a modification of Crown Colony rule, T. A. Marryshow was one of the five members elected to the new Legislative Council. Taylor also notes that, in the 1940s, Marryshow was one of the officers of the Marxist-leaning Caribbean Labour Congress.[32] Marryshow was by no means a lone voice, and the way he influenced others must also be seen as part of the range of ideas circulating in the Caribbean during the first part of the twentieth century. UCLA's African Studies Department writes, for example, that "many modern Caribbean nationalist leaders have acknowledged the importance of Garveyism in their own careers, including T. Albert Marryshow of Grenada; Alexander Bustamante, Sir William Grant, J.A.G. Smith, and Norman Washington Manley of Jamaica, and Captain Arthur Cipriani, Uriah Butler, George Padmore and C.L.R. James of Trinidad."[33] There were, then, several influential schools of thought extant during the period of Hilda Bynoe's childhood. While it is unclear which individuals, apart from Marryshow, had the most influence on her, it is clear that her instincts remained both federalist and pan-Africanist. This appears to have been recognised by pan-Africanist groups. She spoke cordially of these groups and the *Trinidad & Tobago Mirror* reported that she gave an address at the 3rd annual dinner of the African Association of Trinidad & Tobago.[34] She seemed generally interested in the struggles of the working people, although her comments suggest that she did not identify herself with notions of "left" politics or of radical feminism.

As she sat at her home in Diego Martin, Trinidad, Dr Bynoe recalled the days of early anti-colonial agitation and the influence of the known political thinkers of the period, those officially acknowledged and those only known to the communities in which they lived. Alongside her memory of Marryshow, there was a memory of the example given by her mother, and other women of her mother's generation, to Caribbean life generally and to the shaping of her political ideas in particular. She recalled that her mother participated in demonstrations against Colonial Secretary Blood, even while her father, because of his job and his status in the community, could not take part in them.

Given the political and personal history that shaped her, how did Dame Hilda Bynoe think of her role in the Caribbean and in the world? I asked this question in the course of our discussions, and, several times in her responses, Dr Bynoe came back to that question, using it to structure her story, wanting to explain how, as woman, as wife, as mother, as Caribbean person she conceptualised her role in Grenada, in the Caribbean, in the world. Her multi-levelled replies to the question reminds that whatever judgements might be made on her period of office, there are several questions of interest when we consider her story. It is not only about the individual but about how events influenced her, and her influence on the shaping of events. How was it that in a region where males were emerging as the natural inheritors of British male imperial dominance, a woman came to hold the prestigious position of first native governor in her island, and first woman governor anywhere in the British Commonwealth? Was it entirely due to a political decision made by Eric Gairy? What motivated Premier Gairy to make this decision? Was it his own perception of the importance of women's role in Caribbean development? Was it his perception of the importance of the participation of working people (amongst whom he would have numbered her father, T.J. Gibbs and his family), in the politics of the nation? Why was it that a little more than five years after her appointment, the Governor felt personally insulted and unable to continue in her post when demonstrators too casually and, she felt, disrespectfully, associated her name with those of local politicians who "must go"? What was the Governor's role and relationship with the country of which she had become the chief official face? What was her perception of her political role in the Grenadian/Caribbean environment of 1968?

When I was thinking about the anomalies of Dr Bynoe's position as governor, the potential clashes between being the official representative of the British state and her personal views, I was drawn to the story of a nineteenth century Englishman, Thomas Perronet Thompson (1783-1869), a Governor and "political economist, writer, platform speaker and radical MP in his heyday", whose career is described by Michael J. Turner in his article "Raising up Dark Englishmen". Turner describes Thompson as an anti-colonial critic of British imperial policy during a period when such views were very rare.[35] Thompson was the first crown-appointed Governor of Sierra Leone from 1808 to 1810.[36] His avowedly anti-imperial, anti-colonial stance might seem to undermine my implied argument – that, by virtue of her *Caribbean* identification with the land she came to govern, Dame Hilda Bynoe reacted to events in Grenada in a uniquely personal way, that her response as Governor to the events of 1974 reflected the fact that her Caribbean story made her more personally involved than a white expatriate British representative would be. In considering Thompson's attitude to his official role as the Queen's representative in Sierra Leone, Turner argues that "we can learn much more about opinions on empire if we examine the ways in which radicals of Thompson's ilk regarded colonial affairs and questions of race." In his effort to understand his subject, Turner asked, "What influenced Thompson's words and deeds? Why did he emerge as a critic of empire and a champion of the natives at the time of the Indian Mutiny?" Turner's effort to understand Thompson is an effort to understand the times that produced him, the influences on his personal and political background, and how one might situate Thompson within the society of Sierra Leone. I pull the example of Thompson into this discussion because it seems to me that an examination of the life of Dame Hilda Bynoe offers similar kinds of opportunities for understanding and interrogating both the individual and the Caribbean communities that helped to shape her.

Endnotes

1. Representative of the British Crown in a colony or commonwealth state that is not a republic and regards the British monarch as Head of State. The Governor is, in legal terms, the Queen's Representative, appointed on recommendation of the local government. The post is, in effect, more than just ceremonial. In a recent comment on the powers of Governors in those Caribbean states that do not yet have full independence, an article in the August 2004 *New York Amsterdam News* ("British Caribbean Colonies Prepare to tackle Britain", Vol. 95, Issue 38, p.14), notes:

   The premiers or chief ministers of five of Britain's colonies in the Caribbean have decided to challenge the extensive powers British-appointed governors have over their islands and to demand more autonomy to deal with financial and political matters. In the clearest indication yet that the heads are no longer prepared to put up with business as usual, the leaders of the Cayman Islands, volcano-ravaged

Montserrat, Anguilla, the Turks and Caicos Islands, and the British Virgin Islands spent two days in the Caymanian capital last week mainly discussing ways of how to cut the powers of Queen Elizabeth's representative to their islands. Bermuda – the idyllic, temperate, tourist paradise just east of the Carolinas – was the notable absentee, but its Black-led government, now in its second five-year term, has already been talking about moving to gain independence from Britain after 400 years, despite opposition from whites.

The leaders say they want some of the veto powers of governors to be reduced and for Britain to allow them more control over their financial affairs in addition to more leeway on political matters.

For example, Montserrat, a full member of the 15-nation Caribbean Community (Caricom), cannot vote on any foreign affairs matters that Caricom deals with because Britain is still in charge of foreign policy, defence and (to a large extent) its financial affairs as well. On a vote as to whether to recognise Haiti's US-installed administration, Montserrat would have to remain quiet, as Britain's position – rather than the island's – would suffice, a situation that has caused much vexation.

2. For a discussion of Associated Statehood, and the powers of the Governor within that framework, see Masahiro Igarashi, *Associated Statehood in International Law* (The Netherlands: Kluwer Law International, 2002), particularly Chapter 4, "West Indies Associated States." Quotation, p. 134.

3. An Order of chivalry established by the United Kingdom in 1917.

4. Grenada was in French hands between 1652 and 1763 and then between 1779 and 1783. For a discussion, see, for example, Henri Martin, *The Decline of the French Monarchy, Volume 1: History of France from the most remote period to 1789* (Boston: Walker, Fuller & Company, 1866), pp. 535 & 539. (Available both in print and as an e-book). See, too, Gordon Turnbull, *A Narrative of the revolt and insurrection of the French inhabitants in the island of Grenada* (Printed for Arch. Constable at the Cross and sold in London by Vernor & Hood, 1795). Available online as an ebook.

5. Quoted from Merle Collins, *Grenada: A Political History 1950-1979.* Ph.D. thesis, London School of Economics, University of London.

6. Colonial Office Document. CO101/107, desp. No. 138, Keate to Colebrooke, 4 May, 1854. encl. Report on the Blue Book for the year 1853. f. 206. Quoted in Edwina Ashie-Nikoi, *Beating the Pen on the Drum: A Socio-Cultural History of Carriacou, Grenada, 1750-1920* (New York: ProQuest, 2007), p. 262.

7. Alvin Thompson, *The Haunting Past: Politics, Economics and Race in Caribbean Life* (New York: M. E. Sharpe, Inc., 1997), p. 123.

8. Jonathan Pugh and Janet Momsen, *Environmental Planning in the Caribbean* (London: Ashgate Publishing, 2006), p. 25.

9. See, for example, George Brizan, *Grenada: Island of Conflict*. (London: MacMillan, 1998), p. 246; Beverley Steele, *Grenada: A History of its People* (London: McMillan Caribbean, 2003), pp. 239-241; Robin Blackburn, *The Overthrow of Colonial Slavery, 1776-1848* (London: Verso Books, 1988), p. 463.

10. Edwina Ashie-Nikoi, op.cit, p. 299.

11. M.G. Smith, "Stratification in Grenada", *in Blackness in Latin America*, Volume 2, Ed. Whitten & Torres (Indiana University Press, 1998), p. 314.

12. Ibid. p. 318.

13. Ibid., p. 314.

14. *Anthropológica,* Vol. 46 No. 1 (1994), pp. 77-78.

15. Will Kaufman & Heidi Macpherson, *Britain and the Americas: Culture, Politics and Society: Transatlantic Relations* (Santa Barbara: ABC-CLIO Inc., 2005), p. 433.

16. Collins, *Grenada: A Political History*, 1990, pp. 49-50.

17. Eudine Barriteau, "Theorizing Gender Systems and the Project of Modernity in the Twentieth-Century Caribbean, *Feminist Review,* No. 59: *Rethinking Caribbean Difference* (Summer 1998), pp. 186-210.

18. Interview with Gloria Payne-Banfield, November 2011.

19. See Collins, *Grenada: A Political History*, 1990, p. 52.

20. See Collins, *Grenada: A Political History*, p. 53

21. London: The Women's Press, 1987; and revised edition, Leeds: Peepal Tree Press, 2010.

22. M.G. Smith, "Stratification in Grenada", op cit., pp. 313-314.

23. Interview with Mr Caldwell Taylor, November 23, 2010.

24. Nicole Phillip, *Women in Grenadian History 1783-1983* (Kingston, St Augustine, Bridgetown: University of the West Indies Press, 2010), p. 94.

25. Gordon Rohlehr, "The Culture of Williams: Context, Performance, Legacy", *Callaloo* Vol. 20, No. 4, *Eric Williams and the Postcolonial Caribbean: A Special Issue* (Autumn, 1997), pp. 849-888.

26. According to historian Lennox Honychurch, "the French priest Fr Raymond Breton who lived among the "Caribs" recorded the people's own name for themselvea as Calliponam in the women's speech, and Callinago in that of the men". Lennox Honeychurch, *The Dominica Story: A History of the Island* (London: Macmillan Caribbean; Reprint edition, 1995). Some historians today use the phonetic spelling Kalinago instead of Carib. Most people in the region, including Dame Hilda, use the word apparently learned from centuries of European occupation of the region, "Carib".

27. Hilda Bynoe, *I Woke at Dawn* (Port of Spain: Hanz' On Publishers, 1996).

28. For more about Marryshow, see Jill Sheppard, *Marryshow of Grenada: An Introduction* (Letchworth Press, 1987). The book is not now generally available but some information from the text may be found at <http://www.cavehill.uwi.edu/BNCCde/grenada/centre/tam.htm>.

29. Captain Hilary Rudolph Robert Blood (Sir Hilary Blood) was a career colonial Civil Servant. He entered the colonial Civil Service in Ceylon (1920) and served there for a decade before being appointed as Colonial Secretary in Grenada. Between 1942 and 1954, he served the British Colonial Office as Governor (successively) in Gambia, Barbados and Mauritius (The University of Glasgow story, <http://www. universitystory. gla.ac.uk/ww1-biography/?id=1484>).

30. Jan Carew, *Ghosts in Our Blood: With Malcolm X in Africa, England, and the Caribbean* (Chicago, IL: Lawrence Hill Books, 1994).

31. Online publication, *BigDrumNation,* November 19th, 2010. *<http://www.bigdrumnation.org/comments/crowncolony.html>*

32. Interview with Caldwell Taylor, November 18, 2010.

33. "Marcus Garvey and the UNIA" (1995-2010). The Marcus Garvey and UNIA Papers Project, UCLA: UNIA and UCLA African Studies Center. Celebrating 50 Years. 1959-2009. http://www.international.ucla. edu/africa/mgpp/mgunia.asp>. Butler was Tubal Uriah Buzz Butler, a Grenadian who had migrated to Trinidad.

34. *Trinidad & Tobago Mirror*, 13 November 1988.

35. Michael J. Turner, "'Raising up Dark Englishmen': Thomas Perronet Thompson, Colonies, Race, and the Indian Mutiny",

Journal of Colonialism and History, 6:11, (2005), (Project Muse. Article accessed in HTML).

36. Turner, "Raising up Dark Englishmen", op.cit.

CHAPTER TWO
"GETTING THE BEST OF MY ANCESTORS"

Throughout our interviews, Dame Hilda reminded me that the question to which she was responding was: how did you think of your role in the Caribbean and the world? As with every Caribbean story, or indeed any story, there were various cultural and social building blocks that went into the construction of Dr Bynoe's contemporary Caribbean sense of self. But her response began, very consciously, with stories of her ancestors, paternal and maternal.

Maternal Ancestors: Carib and Scottish

Hilda Bynoe's maternal ancestry includes a story, often recounted in the family, of Carib ancestors and particularly of Mayet, Harriet McQuilkin, who lived to be 105.[1] When Mayet died, in or around 1928, her great-granddaughter Hilda was about seven years old.

Dame Hilda's son Roland explains, "My grandmother was a La Touche, my great grandmother was a Redhead, and my great-great grandmother (Mayet) was a McQuilkin whose father was Scottish." Dame Hilda recalls that Mayet, who had never seen a doctor and had treated herself with bush medicine when ill, had perfect vision. Near Mayet's house was a stream and a little pool. Just before her death, Mayet had had a slight cold and was already getting better when she had a dip in the pool, caught viral pneumonia, and died.

Dr Bynoe remembers many gatherings with Mayet and her descendants, grandchildren and great-grandchildren. One memory, in particular, resonates. Assembled in Mayet's yard, the children, asked what they would like to be when they grew up, gave various responses that mostly reflected their rural island experience. Some talked about wanting to be chauffeurs or to work on the estate land near their homes, "in Mr. La Mothe's cocoa", one wanted to be a priest (in fact, he later became a pastor in the Adventist church), their ambitions reflecting the possibilities apparent to them; the child Hilda said she wanted to be a doctor. It was a daring ambition, a self-fulfilling prophecy that her family would never let her forget. All those who were present when the announcement was made, and those who were told about it, let her know that they regarded it as a promise to be fulfilled. With this memory to sustain her, whatever other individuals might think later about their personal roles in the unfolding of her story, Hilda Bynoe was always aware that there were more ancient beginnings to her achievements, beginnings enshrined in her family's – and her community's – perspectives on the role of education in social progress, beginnings witnessed by her family and friends, and by Mayet (Ma Harriet), the Carib ancestor whose life connects to the original Caribbean story.

People in the community around the St Andrew's/St David's area, where the family lived, say they have heard of Mayet. They associate the name with the Gibbs' family story, seeming to know only that Mayet was Carib and that she was somehow connected with the story of T. Joseph Gibbs, Hilda's father, whom they speak of with respect as "Uncle Joe", as someone who owned a shop, who has a place in the story of Grenadian rural society as an "ole-time headmaster for years in Crochu school". One woman assessed that "Uncle Joe's" family were "fairly well off people". They were "not in my bracket when I was growing up", a ninety-year-old woman explained. This description of the Gibbs family in the 1930s and 40s suggests what in the Caribbean might be regarded as an emergent class of black working people who had done well, and who were steadily easing their way into middle-class society. The comment might be measured against the discussion of the folk and social stratification in the period between emancipation in 1838 and Grenada of the 1950s in the previous chapter. The "well off people" would be the ones considered elite, both the rural plantocracy and whites and some of mixed race, perceived to be of superior economic and social status, generally – though not exclusively – resident in St George's, the capital, and environs. The "my bracket" of the speaker suggests a perceived positioning among the less economically privileged folk. The "fairly well off people" may once, ancestrally, have been of the less privileged group, but because of land acquisition, and perhaps education and such factors, they had moved, as the years passed, to a different position up the socio-economic scale.

"My ancestors," Dr Bynoe explained, "came out of Europe, out of

Africa and out of ancient America, a wee bit of all sorts of things and a preponderance of Africa." When I asked about the "wee bits", she responded, "There's Scotland, there is England, there is France – and Ancient America I'm particularly proud of because it was the land of my Carib ancestors." Her response calls to mind Caribbean poet Derek Walcott's conclusion that with all those elements, "either I'm nobody/or I'm a nation".[2] Young Hilda Gibbs's family ensured that she knew she was somebody, and so she claimed various inheritances in the creation of her Caribbean sense of nation.

According to the family narrative, though the oral accounts seem uncertain whether it was Mayet herself or her mother involved, there is a story about one or the other, with her sister, being captured by British sailors either while swimming in Trinidad waters or while walking on the streets of St George's.[3] While the stories handed down through different branches of the family differ in some particulars, one constant is that their ancestor was a young Carib woman captured by British sailors. Since Mayet died in or around 1928 at the age of 105, she would have been born around 1823, and this places the events regarding the story of the capture of Carib maidens some-where either at the beginning of the nineteenth century if the story is about the mother, or in the 1840s if the story is about Mayet herself. According to one family story, the sailors, on their way through the Caribbean with these Carib women captured in Trinidad waters, stopped off in Grenada for food and water. There, the young Carib girls, both good swimmers, escaped. One, Mayet or her mother, made it to shore, but her sister was never heard of again. Another variant tells of Mayet's sister being captured by British sailors on the streets of St George's. Confrontations with European peoples were evidently still dangerous for the original inhabitants of the Carib-bean. The family still speculates that the other sister must have been caught and taken away, but not killed. If so, there may be another half to this story, existing, perhaps, somewhere in Europe or elsewhere in the Americas. Symbolically, the story of the kidnapping remains a powerful motif in this family recounting. It roots the island's first local Governor in the pre-colonial Amerindian heritage of the region.

Mayet McQuilkin married Bozy Redhead, one of the five sons of an Englishman who had migrated to the island. This explains Roland Bynoe's narrative, with which this chapter begins, that his "great grandmother was a Redhead". Dr Bynoe told me, "It's a descendant of the same Redhead, the daughter of another brother, who later married Maurice Bishop.[4] The comment emphasises her understanding of the complex relationships that connect various participants in Caribbean political stories. Dr Bynoe's grandmother, Anne, was one of the twelve children (eleven girls and one boy) of Mayet and her English husband. Anne married a La Touche (and this is confirmed by Roland Bynoe's narrative that his grandmother was a LaTouche) and together they had two children, Eliza, aka Duxie and Louisa (La Touche), who became the mother of Hilda and Josephine. Dr Bynoe speaks of her maternal relatives, descendants of Mayet and Bozy Redhead, as being now resident in several places, in and out of the Caribbean. These residents of the diaspora still have a special relationship with land in and around the boundaries between rural St David's and St Andrew's parishes, Grenada.

Dr Bynoe explained, "My grandmother died very young. She had two children, about a year apart, and after the second child, she died. My mother was the second child. When Mother was about three months old, my grandmother died." Great-grandmother Mayet assumed responsibility for the two girls, Louisa and Eliza, aka Duxie. Louisa married Joseph Gibbs and they had two children, Hilda and Josephine. Duxie, her sister, remembered by her niece as having "long hair down to her waist", married Herbert David and was in Trinidad, en route to Panama to meet her husband, who had travelled there to work on the Panama Canal, when she died of pulmonary tuberculosis. When Duxie died, her children, Enid and Gladys, were taken from Trinidad to Grenada to be part of the Gibbs household of Duxie's sister, Louisa.

Dr Bynoe spoke of these relatives as belonging to one family unit. Her cousin Gladys later had a daughter, Hazel, whom Dr Bynoe adopted, and she was also very close to her aunt Enid. Hazel subsequently travelled to Guyana where she met and married Julien Archer. As Dame Hilda told the stories, both names and details stood out as important and it became clear not only how interwoven are the stories of various families in Grenada's small island community, but also how interconnected are the stories of Caribbean existence. Grenada, Trinidad, Guyana, Panama all feature as part of what is presented as a "Grenada" story because of the demands of "national" identification. Her story was also a practical demonstration of the island dictum that "you never know who you're talking to". It

Louisa LaTouche, Hilda Gibbs' mother, and her cousin.

highlights the importance of the extended family in the society, the family connections created within and between islands and countries. Such stories also help to explain why, in Grenada and other similar small-island (and small country) communities, political tensions – and political relationships generally – are never only about ideology. Known or unknown to outsiders, or sometimes even to other local participants in a political drama, family connections remain an important dynamic influencing individual and, sometimes collective responses to political conflicts. There is often an underlying sense of community knowledge that some family connection is involved in political events, even when these connections cannot be fully detailed. As Dame Hilda recounted these stories, it seemed to me that they suggest that today's "independent" Caribbean nations have ignored their inheritance, undermining their legacy of interwoven histories by focusing on separate postcolonial national identities.

"Mayet," Dr Bynoe told me, "had one son. This son had two sons but one died at a young age. The other, known as Cousin Jose, had a son called Norbert who lost his home during Hurricane Ivan." The mention of Hurricane Ivan is not a gratuitous one. Many individuals connect their personal family stories to details of political events and the hurricanes that regularly transform the landscape – and the Governor's story is no exception. She mentions family events that coincided with "Janet": "The first (family) house went with Hurricane Janet". She was referring to a major hurricane that occurred in 1955 and was probably the preponderant force that organised historical time in the Grenadian imagination until it was displaced by Hurricane Ivan in 2004. This apparently simple detail again situates Dr Bynoe's sensibility as shaped by the natural occurrences of the Caribbean environment.

This kind of extended family and kinship structure, affected as it often is by migration, is quintessentially Caribbean. Indeed, Dr Bynoe's recounting is evidence of what Lara Putnam refers to as the "generative (rather than just communicative) possibilities of narrative", which, she avers, have "particular resonance in the British Caribbean".[5] In other words, these narratives are crucial not only to our understanding of the individual, because they situate her historically, explain her social and political shaping, and her connections with land, personal family and wider Caribbean community, but that such stories have a causative/generative role in the shaping of behaviour. The individual is explained by reference to the past, to ancestry, to land, to location within the community. For instance, when Hilda Bynoe became Grenada's Governor, the fact that she was the daughter of T.J. Gibbs would be an important part of her local identification and the way people responded to her.

T. J. Gibbs's mother, Dr Bynoe's paternal grandmother, had twelve children. On both maternal and paternal sides, the infant mortality rate was high. Her paternal grandmother was called Ma Sese (pronounced SaySay), a Yoruba woman, Dr Bynoe says, revealing her respect for an African heritage. She also referred to Ma Sese's physique as being, in some aspects, Yoruba. Ma Sese, officially Mary Felix, had migrated to Grenada from Dominica in search of land, as did many others who in the post-emancipation period migrated from other islands to Grenada and in particular Trinidad, where land or work was more easily available. In a recent study of migration within the region, Dr Katherine Schmidt notes, "Historically the nature, direction and magnitude of migration in the Caribbean have always been influenced by trends in global and regional socio-economic development."[6] She adds, "After Emancipation in the nineteenth century, the movement of labor to destinations within the region continued." In the post-emancipation period, Dame Hilda explained, the estates in Dominica from which Ma Sese's family came remained in the hands of the large estate owners. The eldest brother of Ma Sese's family, Uncle Lindsay, Lindsay Felix, was the pioneer in the family migrant venture. Uncle Lindsay had gone to Grenada and established his home near what is today the village of Kumar, on the northeast side of the island, close to the border between the parishes of St David's and St Andrew's. "He built his house on the hill, the top of a hill just below Grand Bacolet estate, before the village called Kumar. Kumar did not exist in those days, but I'm identifying it now." Here the narrative gestures towards a more comprehensive local history and one pauses to consider Kumar, this village that "did not exist" in the days when Uncle Lindsay first settled in Grenada. Kumar, which today is synonymous in the Grenadian imagination with Indian identity, "did not exist in those days". When Uncle Lindsay settled in Grenada, Indian settlement had not yet begun to transform the demography of the island. Indians were imported by the British into the Caribbean to substitute for what was described as the post-emancipation loss of African labour. Ron Sookram notes that, "a total of 3,200 Indians were imported into Grenada between 1857 and 1885."[7] Historian George Brizan writes, "in 1881 there were 1,572 Indians in Grenada."[8] Before the settlement of Indians, Kumar did not exist as an entity separate from the village of Grand Bacolet.

On his hillside in Grand Bacolet, Uncle Lindsay worked hard, encouraging his siblings from Dominica to visit and make their home in Grenada. Dr Bynoe mused that the children of this pioneer might be said to have achieved less socially and otherwise, "to have not done as well" as those of his siblings. It is a not unfamiliar story. "He was busy taking care of everybody." It was in response to Uncle Lindsay's call that his sister Mary, Ma Sese, followed his lead and settled in Grenada, where she met and married Sylvester J. Gibbs, a Barbadian who, having quarrelled with his family, had decided to drop the family name and adopt the name Gibbs. The Gibbs family from which Dr Bynoe is descended has no family connection with other families by the name of Gibbs in Grenada. The name Arbuthnot, she believed, was the one that coincided with her Barbados family history.

Here, again, this family story typifies many Caribbean stories. It is not a compact story featuring just one island, but a cross-Caribbean story, with – in this case – strong African threads. The early stories on both maternal and paternal sides involve migration in search of better opportunities; a working people's urge to settle in spaces where it was possible to acquire small plots of land to ensure an independent means of survival; the instability associated with "naming" in Caribbean societies; family narratives that reflect on a history of colonial oppression, and the relationship between all of this and the developing organisation of society in the post-emancipation period. In particular, the stories provide a dynamic example of how Caribbean family patterns have been shaped by migration and how Caribbean migration has been shaped by family patterns.[9] Further, a reading of Mary Chamberlain's *Family Love*,[10] and Lara Putnam's assessment of this work, helps situate Dr Bynoe's concern to locate herself in her extended family, including relatives with whom she may no longer have contact, but whose stories are important to her construction of self and, importantly for our story, relevant to her construction of the world in which she was to operate as a governor.

Lara Putnam, discussing *Family Love*, draws attention to Chamberlain's conclusion that "Families are micro-societies of their own, with their own histories and cultures, creating their own dynamics and ethos, continuities and ruptures, constantly evolving to accommodate growth and change – of individual family members and of the family as a unit."[11]

Thus, in one strand of the story, Dr Bynoe drew attention to her paternal grandmother, Ma Sese's struggle to ensure her children's success, her going to work at difficult jobs so that her children would be able to advance socially and economically. She noted how her father appreciated his mother's struggles, how, "as soon as my father could, he built (his mother) a cottage." She recalled the cottage, the family house, plum trees, and a special relationship between her father's family and the area around St David's and St Andrew's parishes. Other members of the family had acquired lots in northeastern villages like Mama Cannes, (what is today) Kumar and other areas.

This structuring of the narrative, Dr Bynoe's concern to give details both about the land and about her extended family, suggest that she is very conscious of her story as coming from a particular ideological base. As Anthony Maingot has noted, "West Indian peasant ownership (is) synonymous with freedom." Maingot adds that it is "a story as old as the Haitian revolution…"[12] It is a story pertinent to political organisation notably because the evidence is that the Grenadian peasantry and working people are less interested in any ideological reasons for reorganising of society than in the practical value, social and economic, of land ownership. While Dr Bynoe's maternal family story is bound up with the Amerindian inhabitants of the Caribbean lands (to describe them as "owners" would seem inconsistent with Amerindian values) and with her great-grandmother Mayet who "was never a slave", as well as with the migration of British people who were migrants seeking their fortune in the Caribbean; her paternal family story features Africans who had been taken to the Caribbean during the period of enslavement and who, in the post-emancipation period, moved from one island to another in search of better opportunities and, more specifically, in search of land on which to settle. Because it was easier for the ex-slaves to get grants of land in Grenada, as noted above, her father's maternal ancestors moved from Dominica to Grenada. Then they moved again, back to Dominica, to Trinidad, to Panama, to Maracaibo in Venezuela. All of this is important to an understanding of Dr Bynoe's insistent belief in Caribbean integration, notwithstanding the fact that Caribbean political organisation in the post-independence period has run counter to the federalist instincts of politicians such as T.A. Marryshow.

Inevitably, this sense of her origins conditioned Governor Bynoe's responses to attitudes encountered during her period of political office. Personal narratives are embedded in and are used to explain economic and socio-political realities. Dr Bynoe never spoke in general terms about the various members of the family, but invariably named the individuals and their stories.

> "Datchik got his piece of land and worked it. Paren got his piece of land and worked it. They had this tradition, even in those early days. In those days, too, people wanting to emigrate would lease their piece of land for cash to pay their expenses. They would lease it to you for two years, five years. You would reap the land, and you would purchase it in the end, if they didn't come back, or you would lease land again and eventually you would own the land. Some of my uncles acquired land and married and settled down and they had their families. And my aunts, two of them – one is May Regis's grandmother who married a man with a piece of land and had his children."

There are several facets to the story that Dame Hilda told. It was about the relationship with land developed in the post-emancipation period as a means towards personal freedom; it was about the fact that ownership often came in small lots slowly and precariously acquired; about why education meant so much to working people especially in the period following full adult suffrage, when it became progressively clear that working people of various races could inherit the highest offices in the land; the place of religion and the church in shaping the values and identities of individuals and groups; how family relationships are woven into the social fabric of the community; and the particular role of generations of women, exemplified by Ma Sese and Mayet, in ensuring that their children first of all survived, and then, subsequently, made it up the social ladder. Of the struggles of her paternal grandmother, Ma Sese, for her children, Dr Bynoe said:

> "When she should be sending them out to work, she decided that she herself would go out to work. She went to the Grand Bacolet estate as a labourer at that time of her life, and then, of course, as soon as my father could, he built her a cottage."

These are memories not only of the self-sacrificing mother but also of the dutiful son, aware and respectful of the sacrifice made, and, importantly, the role of the usually white-owned agricultural estate in the lives of the working people.

Dr Bynoe mentions not only the cottage built by her father but also the trees around the cottage – plum, sugar apple, sapodilla – and the fact that the trees on her family land were often the markers of graves. Her ancestors were buried on that land, because "only the very rich built tombstones". The tree as a symbolic marker of the resting places of ancestry gives a particular resonance to Dr Bynoe's later recounting that when the announcement of her governorship was made in 1968, she was "on a plum tree". That positioning – "on a plum tree" – is itself a story. When the announcement was made, Dr Bynoe was ingesting her ancestors and sharing with them an achievement they had helped to produce. The land owned by the family is a repository of ancestral memory. Dr Bynoe remembered realising as a little girl that there were graves in that place where the plum trees were planted, plum trees that were monuments to the ancestors.

> "...and we had a beautiful yellow plum orchard down there and I remember as a child getting these plums and I used to say I'm going to be clever because I'm getting the best of my ancestors."

When I mentioned this part of the story to Caldwell Taylor, his observation was that in more ways than one the Governor was defying tradition, for it was at one time a popular belief, no doubt influenced by various religious stories and certainly by the Bible story of Eve's role in the garden of Eden, that girls could "spoil" a plum or other fruit tree, "make the fruit sour" by perching on the branches and eating the fruit.

The Governor's family story also confirmed that religious institutions frequently structure community activities. In this part of Grenada, the Catholics had their cemetery to which others did not have access, so that working people who were not Catholics had to make other arrangements for the disposal of their dead. The importance of Christian denominations in this story is also a testament to patterns that unfolded during the post-emancipation period when the Roman Catholic and Anglican churches competed in the conversion of African peoples to Christianity. When the Indians settled in Kumar, and other places later, it was the Presbyterian churches who were (as elsewhere in the Caribbean) more active in their conversion. As Dame Hilda reported:

> "There was a piece of land in the area going down by the sea which had belonged to Mayet and her husband. It belonged to the family. They were not Catholics and the cemetery was always a Catholic cemetery and so they had their own private cemetery and that is where the cemetery was."

This then is a story that resonates with a sense of belonging to and understanding of the land and the complex relationship to it of the people who occupy it. These personal understandings moved with Hilda Bynoe in her professional life, as first the doctor and then the governor, to help shape her interaction with the wider community. For example, in celebrating the particular contributions of the women on both sides of her family, Dr Bynoe sees them as part of a wider set of women's values. Ma Sese, she said, was

> "typical of the African women that I know, that I learnt to know as I grew up, and in the generations, in my office, and so on, in Guyana and wherever I worked – the African woman, similar to the Indian woman in the sense of having the responsibility and having the ambition that my child must get a stage ahead of me."

It is evident that when Dr Bynoe encountered people in her office she saw them in historical perspective, always conscious of the circumstances of their existence – and in particular the circumstances of Caribbean women on their journeys towards achievement not only for themselves, but for the families for which they felt themselves responsible. This was a historical perspective to be found more in the oral tradition than in scribal history. As the Caribbean scholar Rhoda Reddock states:

> ...even while women's contribution to wage work and participation in labour struggles was not acknowledged in mainstream labour scholarship, the oral tradition and other sources reveal a central contribution by women and their children to many of the labour struggles of the late nineteenth century and early twentieth century of the Caribbean region.[13]

Notions of Diaspora and Globalisation[14]

Joseph Harris writes that the concept of the African diaspora as a field of study "gained momentum from 1965 when the International Congress of African Historians convened in Tanzania and included in its program a session entitled, "The African Abroad or the African Diaspora".[15] However, the reality of what lay behind this discursive term had existed long before this period. And whilst the term first gained currency as a mode of description for the historical experience of exile of the Jewish people, the word first came into general usage for the African experience of dispersal some time between the mid-1950s and the mid-1960s. As George Shepperson notes:

> Who first used this expression, I do not know; and I wish very much that someone would attempt the difficult task of tracing the employment of the Greek word for dispersal – which, until it began to have the adjective *African* or *black* attached to it, was used largely for the scattering abroad of the Jews.[16]

Dame Hilda, in our conversations, was clearly conscious of various kinds of diaspora experience in the formation of her own consciousness. She spoke of the "African women" and "the Indian women" encountered in her offices, stressing the points of origin of these Caribbean people. It became clear, too, that to Dame Hilda, the Grenadian story was also Dominican, Trinidadian and Barbadian, and that this is a core Caribbean phenomenon. Indeed, the post-slavery travelling between countries of the ex-enslaved replicates that of the original Amerindian inhabitants moving from mainland and through the islands, and that of European interlopers who moved from one island to another (often bringing their enslaved Africans with them) in the search for greater opportunities, or when circumstances, such as in Santo Domingo in 1790s, caused European colonists to flee to safer shores.

Dr Bynoe's narrative highlights, in a very personal way, the essentially interlocking nature of Caribbean existence as demonstrated through the experience of the wider Bynoe family. Not all the brothers who followed Uncle Lindsay stayed in Grenada. One member of the family, Ma Sese's oldest son and T.J. Gibbs's brother, returned to Dominica, and of Dominica she said, "My father went *back*, when his brother died." The family responsibility was not only to the Grenadian space but also to family members who "went back" to another Caribbean island. Dominica became an integral part of the notion of home. An important part of Ma Sese's legacy to Grenada, Dominica and the Caribbean was that, as Dr Bynoe noted, "she gave her children, girls and boys, the maximum of elementary education. That is what she could give them and she gave it to all of them."

Caribbean people living in countries such as England or the United States maintain a concept of an absent, original home-space and today, when there are discussions of diaspora, these discussions tend to focus on that dispersal from developing to developed countries. Dr Bynoe's story is a reminder that, just as there were dispersals of African people across Africa, highlighted, for example, in E. Kamau Brathwaite's *Masks* (1968), the second part of his trilogy, *The Arrivants*,[17] before the forced dispersal across the Atlantic into the Americas, so Caribbean people – African, Indian, Amerindian and the various admixtures of these peoples – have continued to migrate within and across the Caribbean, establishing diasporic identities long before the increased emigration to sites outside of the region that followed the 1939-1945 World War. In contemporary Trinidad, for instance, it has been estimated that one in three Trinidadians came from elsewhere in the Caribbean.[18]

In Dr Bynoe's recounting, "My father went back" constructs Grenada as what today might be described as a Dominican diaspora for the family of Uncle Lindsay. "My father went to Dominica to see that his brother was properly buried and to see if he had any wife… and there was no connection left that he had to worry about or bring back home or anything like that." In this case, "home" is transposed onto the Grenada experience. Dr Bynoe remembers that her father returned from Dominica with "a marble topped table" that is "still there, with a little crack", in the family house in Crochu. A tangible bit of the Dominican story sits, symbolically, in the Grenadian home space.

This sense of intra-regional migration lies behind Dr Bynoe's commitment to a federal future for the region. Not only was her maternal great-great grandmother stolen from "Trinidad waters", but, in reverse, her paternal grandfather, Mr. Gibbs, "a tailor by trade", travelled to Trinidad in search of better employment opportunities because he was not earning enough for his family to survive off his trade and their five acres of "mountain land" in Grenada. In

Trinidad, he found employment as an estate overseer and, although he kept contact with and later returned to his Grenada family, he fathered a child in Trinidad. As Dr Bynoe said, "My father acknowledged her."

Later, when Dr Bynoe travelled through the United States, she met her relatives, Mayet's descendants, in New York. Another thread of the story takes family members to Maracaibo and to Panama.[19] While nationalism might constrict family borders, members of the family inhabit and are citizens of the world, and were so long before the world came to speak of itself in global terms. As historian Mary Chamberlain notes, globalisation is not a new concept; it lies at the heart of modernity. She writes:

> International migration… strikes at the heart of nationhood and the nation state… International migrants are by definition global people whose horizons and allegiances, education and enterprise, family and friendship are both portable and elastic. What, finally, unsettles about international migration is that it internationalises the nation-state and globalises identity… And few, if any, people are more global and more migratory than those from the Caribbean.[20]

It is a fact that Caribbean governments have been forced to recognise. Today, throughout the region, governments are turning more obviously to engage the ideas of citizens in the diaspora in the business of national development. Dr Bynoe's story reminds us that Caribbean family economics and family organisation have long quietly acknowledged what governments, perhaps hampered by a nationalist narrative, have been slower to engage.

Endnotes

1. Amerindian or Native American. One of the peoples met by the Europeans when they invaded the Caribbean. Recently, the group known as the "Caribs" in Dominica, announced that they were officially going to name themselves "Kalinagos". Kalinago is thought to have been the original name for the Carib peoples, before the Europeans named them "Carib", meaning "cannibal".

2. Derek Walcott, "The Schooner *Flight*", *The Star-Apple Kingdom* (London: Cape, 1980), p. 4.

3. The first inhabitants of the country today known as Trinidad & Tobago were the Kalinago peoples. In 1498, Columbus happened upon the island, named it La Trinidad and claimed it for Spain. The first significant but never very sizeable Spanish settlements were in the 1590s. In 1797, Britain invaded and took the island from Spain. The family story of the capture of Mayet's mother and sister in Trinidad waters may date from these days of the second wave of British imperial incursion into the region.

4. Maurice Bishop was a member of the New Jewel Movement, which ousted Prime Minister Eric Gairy from office in the "British" Caribbean's first revolutionary overthrow. Bishop was Prime Minister of Grenada from 1979 to 1983. In that year, he and several colleagues were murdered in internecine party strife. Following these events, the United States invaded Grenada.

5. Lara Putnam, "Caribbean Kinship from Within and Without", *History Workshop Journal,* Issue 56 (Autumn 2008), pp. 279-288.

6. Dr Katherine Schmidt, "Migration in the Caribbean", ECLAC Subregional Headquarters for the Caribbean (2010). <http://www.slideshare. net/egfred/migration-in-the-caribbean-dr-katherine-schmidt>.

7. Ron Sookram, The Indian Community in Grenada (Germany: VDM Verlag, 2009), p. 12. Sookram quotes George Roberts and Joycelyn Byrne, "Summary Statistics on Indenture and Associated Migration Affecting the West Indies, 1834-1918", *Population Studies* 20 (1966), p. 129. See also Ron Sookram, "Grenada in Contemporary Historiography", *Small Axe* - Number 22, Volume 11, Number 1, (February 2007), pp. 156-163.

8. See George Brizan, *Grenada Island of Conflict* (London: MacMillan Caribbean, 1997), p. 245.

9. Lara Putnam poses these questions ("Caribbean Kinship", p. 282) in her 2008 discussion of Mary Chamberlain's work on Caribbean kinship.

10. Mary Chamberlain, *Family Love in the Diaspora: Migration and the Anglo-Caribbean Experience* (New Jersey: Transaction Publishers, Memory and Narrative Series, 2009).

11. Putnam, p. 286.
12. Both are quotations from Anthony Maingot, "Review: Coming to Terms with the 'Improbable Revolution'", *Journal of Interamerican Studies and World Affairs*, Volume 27, Number 3 (Autumn 1985), pp. 77-190.
13. Constance Sutton, ed., *Revisiting Caribbean Labour: Essays in Honour of O. Nigel Bolland* (Kingston: Ian Randle Publishers, 2005), p. 21.
14. For further comments on the recurring theme of diaspora, see above pp. 37-39.
15. For a discussion, see Joseph Harris, *Global Dimensions of the African Diaspora* (Washington: Howard University Press, Second Edition, 1993), pp. 3-4, "Diaspora as Concept and Method".
16. George Shepperson, "The African Abroad or the African Diaspora", in T.O. Ranger (ed.) Emerging Themes of African History (Nairobi, 1968), p. 152.
17. Kamau Brathwaite, *The Arrivants* (Oxford: Oxford University Press, 1973).
18. See the International Organization for Migration <http://www.iom.int/cms/en/sites/iom/home/where-we-work/americas/central-and-north-america-and-th/trinidad-and-tobago.html>
19. See notes to Chapter Two for references to Panama and to Wilfred Little and the dissemination of ideas in the diaspora.
20. Mary Chamberlain, *Caribbean Migration: Globalised Identities* (London: Routledge, Taylor & Francis e-library, 2002), p. 1.

CHAPTER THREE

EDUCATION AND THE SOCIAL CONTEXT

Many Caribbean narratives attest to the importance of education in the achievement of the aspirations of Caribbean working people. Education presented – and continues to present – the possibility of escape from the fields and low-paying service occupations and movement toward the professions. The child Hilda Gibbs had early declared her ambition to attain one of the most prestigious positions available in her island. On her way to that goal, she worked at other professions accessible from Grenada's education system. She was, not unusually, attracted to teaching, a profession that afforded both a respectable status and the opportunity to play an important community role in service to others. In *Women in Grenadian History,* Nicole Phillip records Dame Hilda's earlier career:

> Although she sat and passed the Senior Cambridge School Certificate Examination in 1936, she was unable to study abroad because she did not win the one island scholarship that entitled the student to free university education abroad. With no money available to fulfil her dreams to become a doctor, she became a teacher. In 1940, she won one of the Colonial Development and Welfare Fund Scholarships. These scholarships were awarded in the wake of the report made by the Moyne Commission in 1939 on the state of the Caribbean colonies including education.[1]

The word "abroad" is not to be lightly dismissed. Acquiring further education meant having to go abroad. In those years, there was no University of the West Indies, so university education typically meant travel to Britain.

Concerning the context within which her education and early employment as a teacher are to be understood, Dame Hilda explained:

> There was no formal training for teachers in my childhood. The best
> students became monitors, then came the pupil teachers, the assistant
> teachers, the headmaster. My father went through that system and
> remained headmaster in Crochu[2] R.C. School all his life.

Dr Bynoe's mother was a teacher before she married T. Joseph
Gibbs, as was her older sister Josephine (Phine).

Her father, Dr Bynoe said, was "the father of the village and was
known as 'Uncle Joe' to all." He became a politician, landowner and
entrepreneur. He owned the village bus, "Excelsior", and burnt coral
stone into white lime for the building industry. He also owned the
village shop and a factory that manufactured "cola" (sweet drink). He
became a justice of the peace and prepared wills for people. If he was
an important village figure, so too, Dr Bynoe said, was her mother,
"part of everything", working alongside her husband. Typically in
this partnership, "Uncle Joe" was the Secretary of the La Sagesse, St
David's Race Club and his wife ran the bar.[3]

Hilda Gibbs learned to read early and "do sums", but she hated
spelling. She credits her godfather, Cyril Sylvester, popularly known
as C.I. Sylvester, Grenada's first black inspector of schools, with
responsibility for her love of mathematics. "He taught me mathematics and taught me so well that I understood it. I couldn't spell but
I could do sums." She had bouts of malaria, she recalled, "like
everyone else", and somewhere during those years she also con-
tracted polio. She remembered that her father carried her in his arms
to his school because she couldn't walk. She remembered visits to
doctors, but at the time there seems to have been no confirmed
diagnosis of polio. That was to come later, when, as a medical student,
she decided to find out what had actually been the source of this
childhood illness that had made both parents very concerned. The
story suggests her early consciousness of a need for better medical
facilities for the working poor and the aspiring and better paid
working class of colonial Grenada.

Hilda Gibbs was eleven, approaching twelve, when, in 1933, she
passed the scholarship examination for high school.[4] In the 1930s,
unless their children won a scarce scholarship, even secondary school
education was an expensive luxury for the working people of the
Caribbean, and Hilda was one of the fortunate few to win a scholarship. She went to the St Joseph's Convent High School. Opened in
1875, the Convent provided an elite education for those who could

afford it, or who won a coveted scholarship. At the time when Hilda Gibbs was a student, St Joseph's Convent (or the Convent as the high school was popularly known) had both day pupils and boarders. Dr Bynoe names other Grenadians who were her contemporaries there – Constance Fletcher, a day pupil, and the Rapier sisters, Thelma, Florence and Irva, who were boarders. Connie, Florence (Faye) and Hilda were good friends and came to be known at school as "The Three Musketeers". Again, the names in this narrative are important; they would be recognised as belonging to either members of the established Grenada middle class those or emerging into it. The friendships cemented while Hilda Gibbs was at school were to last a lifetime.

I asked about her influences and she named her parents as unques-tionably positive influences in the unfolding of her life story. There were others. There was, for example, J.W. Fletcher, father of her high school friend Constance, known in Grenada as an "old-time head-master". Dr Bynoe recalled: "I used to go there (to his home in St George's, located at the top of Market Hill, not far from the St Joseph's Convent High School) and listen to his stories." J.W. Fletcher was the first person to tell her about Julien Fedon, a mixed-race French planter who fought against the British in 1795-96, and who must be considered one of Grenada's national heroes.[5] At the Fletcher home, she also met John Watts, later founder of the Grenada National Party, which emerged to challenge Eric Gairy for national power in 1955. Watts was then a schoolboy boarder at the Fletchers' house.

After Hilda passed her Cambridge exams at St Joseph's Convent, because her family "was having problems with money", it was decided that she should begin working. Her godfather, C.I. Sylvester's effective teaching of mathematics served her well when she later travelled for work to San Fernando, Trinidad. During our interview, Dr Bynoe mused that "if I hadn't been set on medicine, I could have become a mathematics teacher." She also named "Cousin Tisha", Head Mistress at Pomme Rose Roman Catholic School, as another influential figure in her life, someone who became a mother figure to her after her own mother's sudden death when she was fourteen. "She had invited my mother on a (road) trip with the children from her school and my mother got killed in an accident during that trip."

She told the story quietly, but the death of her mother had clearly been devastating. Later, she wrote movingly about this period of her life in a poem, "The Meaning of Grief",[6] which details in simple language the closeness of the relationship with her mother, how the young girl away at boarding school in St George's looked forward to her mother's visits, and the way her mother's passing overturned her world and made her look more closely at tiny details in the world around her. The setting for the poem is the environs of her home in rural Crochu:

> I saw the people
> Big crowds of people
> Standing about,
> Sitting around
> Filling up the yard
> Overflowing into the road.
> Many were sobbing aloud.
>
> Some called out to me
> As they saw me arriving.
> I kept hoping and praying:
> Knowing
> But not believing
> Refusing to believe.
> Could she really be dead?
>
> Throughout the long night
> I wandered around
> One lost little girl
> Wandering around
> Not understanding
> Not understanding at all
> Why God should have taken her
> My own dear Mother
> So needed, so loved.
>
> Early next morning
> The telephone began ringing
> It kept on ringing all day
> People kept on asking for her
> Her many friends and some others

Who did business with her.
I had to tell them
I had to say it.
"She is dead."

Buses passed by as usual
Next morning
On their way into town.
I stood there by the gate
Watching them stopping
Some not stopping
People getting out
People getting in
Just the same
The same as before.

Then along came the mail-bus
And Thelma calling me
And handing me shoes
My new shoes
Left behind in school.

My friend had been wearing them
(I was wearing hers)
Stretching them out to fit me
When Enid came to call me,
It was just last night.

Mother had bought them
A little too small
Just the other day
And now she was gone
Gone away
Leaving me.
No tears were left me.

I listened quite numb
To the chanting of the priest
The praying of the people.

I stood there at her graveside
Stood watching
While they placed her in a hole
"Dust to dust and ashes to ashes."

It was like a knife – this grief
Plunging deep
Deep down within me
Turning and twisting my guts
Making griping, aching pain
A terrible choking pain.

Tears came afterwards
In floods came the tears
During the days and the weeks
The many long nights
The months afterwards.

I missed her kisses, her hugs
The many scoldings, long talks
Kind words and advice
I needed so much.
And no-one could give them.
Not quite like her.

I missed her cooking
Blessings
Sharing in her prayers
Anancy and the other stories
She told so well.

Saturday mornings
Visits to my Convent School.
I missed all the laughing together
The singing and the dancing
Just the chatting together
Happy times together

The sound of her voice
The sight of her face
All the many things
A mother shares with her child
Girl child
And just growing up
To face the many problems of life.

Mother-love. Friendship
The giving and the sharing
All the loving, forgiving
Hugging
Special childhood gifts
I lost them one night
And learnt the meaning of Grief.

The trees were swaying
And gentle breezes blowing
Early morning
The next morning
Birds were singing
Butterflies flittering
From flower to flower.
A telephone line.

And two Sissy-birds
Now perched on the line.
Same old telephone line
Just hours before
had carried the news
That shattered my world.
Teaching me
The meaning of Grief.

After her mother's death, the child Hilda cried constantly:

"I loved her dearly, and all my life afterwards, there were dreams of
her. In the first dream, she was angry, very, very angry. I heard a knock
at the upstairs door and there she was in her red and white apron.
'Why don't you let me rest?' she said. After that, all my other dreams

were beautiful. We were happy together, visiting each other. We would chat together and were happy. I always knew she would go and come back many, many times. And then, one night in the dream, she said, 'I am not coming back' and there she was, you know. A long, long ladder appeared and she climbed and climbed. I saw her climbing, until I could see neither her nor her ladder anymore. She had gone into Heaven. I have dreamt of her no more."

This quiet story about death, resurrection and a very catholic assumption into heaven suggests both the influence of the child's catholic education and a period of intense psychological trauma for one who had lost her mother at this early age.

After her mother's death, Hilda's father became father and mother for her. She recalled:

"He even started giving me castor oil and vermifuge for the worms.[7] Of course, that did not last for long. I went back to the Convent. I was a boarder. Sister Phine, Enid, Nona and Gladys all helped to bring me up."

The older sister and extended female family were important as nurturers at this particularly difficult time. After his wife's death, T. Joseph Gibbs never married again. Hilda's elder sister, Phine, and her cousins, adopted the role of female caretakers, and the Convent played a supplementary role.

At the time, there were two girls' secondary schools in Grenada – the St Joseph's Convent and the Anglican High School. Both were important in the education and socialisation of the country's young women. People I spoke to from among the Grenadian working people told me that, "the convent of yesterday was not like today. You had to be *you* to be in convent yesterday." The implication was that only people of a certain social bracket, or those from among the working people lucky enough to win a scholarship to this prestigious institution, would have the benefit of a Catholic secondary education. The fact that there were only two girls' secondary schools and two boys' secondary schools and that three of those were run by the Catholic and Anglican churches testifies to the importance of the religious denominations in the shaping of the community in the post-emancipation period. As Kenneth Ramchand details in his seminal work *The West Indian Novel and its Background* (1967): "included in the Act of Emancipation (1833), was a resolution to provide 'upon liberal and comprehensive principles for the religious and moral Education of the Negro population to be emancipated'."[8] Ramchand notes that "The resultant Negro Education Grant was allocated to the different religious bodies already at work in the colonies…"[9] As a result, in Grenada and elsewhere, the churches' pre-existing position gave them a significant head-start in the organisation of education in Caribbean post-emancipation societies. Regarding the situation for girls at the St Joseph's Convent, Nicole Phillip notes:

> St Joseph's Convent was predominantly a girls' school, although there were a few boys enrolled. Scholars at the Convent paid two pounds per annum. The fees were three pounds a month for boarders; four shillings for day scholars under age seven, and eight shillings for those over age seven; and eight shillings extra for drawing and painting and ten shillings for music.[10]

By winning a scholarship to the Convent, Hilda Gibbs had gained access to an education that would have been beyond her family's means.

As noted above, after she graduated from St Joseph's Convent, Hilda Gibbs went to Trinidad. T. Joseph Gibbs operated comfortably in the role that Caribbean mothers are traditionally said to perform for their children. Not wealthy, but with a respectable, now arguably lower middle-class status as an entrepreneur and headmaster of a primary school, he was in some ways ahead of his time, ensuring that his daughter would advance socially and economically. On 3rd September, 1939, on her sister Phine's birthday, on the day that Britain entered the second world war, Hilda Gibbs and her friend Connie Fletcher, accompanied by their fathers, arrived in Trinidad on their way to the convent at San Fernando, in South Trinidad. In Trinidad, they were met by Gibbs Annisette, a solicitor and friend of the Fletchers. Later, Hilda would have another reason to remember 3rd September. Eight years later it would be the date of her wedding.

The San Fernando Convent, in the south of the island, was a newly opened Catholic secondary school for girls. Moving from one British colony to another, and from one Catholic convent community to another, was moving from the known to the known, so it was an easy transition. Both schools occupied much the same place in the colonial class structure of their islands. Connie Fletcher was a specialist teacher of English and music and Hilda Gibbs was a specialist teacher in mathematics, teaching maths to all classes, and occasionally teaching history. As Dame Hilda reported later, both she and Connie were able and keen to teach.

For two years, Hilda Gibbs and Connie Fletcher continued to work under informal contracts at the San Fernando Convent. They were both very successful teachers and Dr Bynoe remembers that she had excellent results, especially in her second year of teaching.

During these years in Trinidad, her political education developed. As she explained, "I was exposed to the influence of (my cousin) David Pitt and his mother. There was the West Indies National Party (WINP), formed in 1942,[11] of which Pitt, Albert Gomes,[12] and Patrick Solomon[13] were members. I also became an active member. So my interest in politics was there. Not that I ever wanted to be a politician." She recalls that Grenada's T.A. Marryshow had the support of the W.I.N.P. Those were the days, she recalled, when women did not have the vote until they were thirty, although, she says, "I didn't know it then."

These years in Trinidad were not without problems for young Hilda Gibbs. "At about the end of my second year, there was a mild epidemic of German measles and I became ill. The nuns tried to send me to Gertie Redhead, Dr David Pitt's[14] mother, but David feared for his patients and the nuns sent me to the Annisettes[15] in Port of Spain". The Annisettes were the friends of the Fletchers who had met the young people when they first arrived in Trinidad. "Aunt Julia" Annisette took young Hilda in and cared for her until she was well. When Hilda's father was apprised of the situation, he was grateful to the Annisettes but angry with the nuns at San Fernando, in whose care he had left his daughter. He went to Trinidad, collected his daughter's belongings and the two returned to Grenada, where Hilda taught school at her alma mater, St Joseph's Convent, until she left for England to study medicine.

These stories of the movements of Hilda Gibbs and her family in the 1930s and 40s provide some insight into the shaping of those who moved from the better-off and aspiring sections of the working class into the Caribbean middle class. In the Grenada situation, these terms must be understood with reference to previous discussions of the folk and the elite, because this was a family that, as it moved up the ranks socially and economically, remained close to its experience amongst those described by M.G. Smith as "the folk". They understood and remained sensitive to the needs and goals of the people they had come from. The Gibbses belonged to a section of the working class which had opportunities for land ownership and education, and was positioning itself to inherit the future.

Trained by nuns and priests, some of Hilda Gibbs' contemporaries moved into the church. Her friend, Connie Fletcher, eventually became a nun and joined the Convent in Port-of-Spain. The two, though, remained friends, sharing family and community rituals. Connie Fletcher's youngest sister is Dr Bynoe's goddaughter, another instance of the complex interweaving of social relationships in a small community. People who had shared rituals at school and in their early working lives tended to remain connected, and this had implications for various types of social and political organisation.

Some years after their Trinidad experience, Connie Fletcher returned to Grenada and opened a second Convent school at Grenville, St Andrew's. Years later, after Dame Hilda Bynoe's period as Governor came to end, after Prime Minister Eric Gairy was ousted and a revolutionary government took office, Connie Fletcher had risen to the position of Mother Superior in Grenada. By this period, those who had been trained by the expatriate (usually Irish) nuns were moving into positions of leadership in the religious institutions in their communities, another instance of the way in which, politically and socially, West Indians were inheriting positions of leadership from the colonials.

After teaching school in Grenada in the early 1940s, Hilda Gibbs won a scholarship to study medicine. This scholarship came as a result of the recommendations regarding education made by the Moyne Commission (the West India Royal Commission), which after the upsurge of labour unrest, mass demonstrations and social disorder which swept much of the Anglophone Caribbean between 1935-1937, was sent to the Caribbean in 1938-39 to report on social and economic conditions. Under various headings, the report made recommendations for improvement in the lives of the people.[16] One recommendation was that more scholarships to higher education be awarded to students throughout the British Caribbean. T. Joseph Gibbs had been applying to various universities in the United States and England, trying to ensure that when the war ended his daughter would have a place to continue her education and work towards achieving her dreams. Eventually, Dr Bynoe recounted, she found a place at London University.

Later, when Dr Bynoe was appointed Governor, she had family and other connections with the local populace. She was intimately connected to the story of land ownership, had a personal understanding of the role of the churches in education, and had close relationships with members of the religious orders who were in control of education. She was never likely to be a disinterested participant in the political processes of the country.

Endnotes

1. Nicole Laurine Phillip, *Women in Grenadian History 1783-1983.* (Kingston: University of the West Indies Press, 2010), p. 68.
2. Crochu, a village in the parish of St Andrew's, Grenada, on the eastern side of the island, is close to the border between St Andrew's and St David's parishes.
3. Horse racing at La Sagesse, St David's, was a Grenadian institution inherited from the British. The practice faded out in the 1960s.
4. This examination – given fictional treatment in the work of many Caribbean writers, including in George Lamming's *In the Castle of My Skin* (1953) and in V.S. Naipaul's *A House for Mr Biswas* (1961) – allowed the brightest children to be given a free secondary school education. It was an important rite in the lives of Caribbean children, but for the majority a disappointing one.
5. See Edward Cox, "Fedon's Rebellion 1795-96: Causes and Consequences", *The Journal of Negro History.* Vol. 67, No. 1, Spring 1982.
6. Dame Hilda Bynoe, *I Woke at Dawn* (Trinidad: Hanz' On Publishers, 1996), pp.101-106
7. Castor oil and a vermifuge were then the standard treatment to give young people an internal cleanse ("a wash out"), especially during the holidays.
8. Kenneth Ramchand, *The West Indian Novel and its Background* [1967] (Kingston: Ian Randle Publishers, reprint 2004, p. 3.)

9. Ramchand, op.cit.

10. Nicole Laurine Phillip, *Women in Grenadian History 1783-1983*, p. 69.

11. For more on the West Indies National Party, see Ray Kiely, *The Politics of Labour Development in Trinidad* (Kingston: University of the West Indies Press, 1996), p. 84.

12. In the 1930s, Albert Gomes, a Trinidadian of Portuguese descent, along with another Portuguese, Alfred Mendes, and with C.L.R. James, became involved in the publication of a radical literary magazine, *The Beacon*. For more on Gomes, see a Caribbean Community Secretariat (CARICOM) entry at <http://www.caricom.org/jsp/projects/personalities/albert_gomes.jsp?menu=projects>.

13. Patrick Solomon later became Trinidad's Minister of Education between 1956-60. A 1928 Island Scholar, he studied medicine in Ireland and Scotland. Between 1939 and 1943, he worked in the Leeward Islands Medical Service.

14. The Pitts were descended from the Redhead family into which Mayet married. See above, pp. 34-38.

15. Dr Bynoe mentioned that Aunt Julia Annisette in later years married Mr Peter Bynoe's uncle, Cyril Joseph.

16. The Report of the Commission was not published until 1945 (*West India Royal Commission Report,* HMSO, 1945). Hilda Gibbs left the country on scholarship before 1945 but after the visit of the Commission. It is likely that colonial governments began implementing recommendations of the Commission before the Report was actually officially available in print.

CHAPTER FOUR

TRAVELLING IN WAR-TIME

Hilda Gibbs had reached Trinidad to teach at the San Fernando Convent when England entered the Second World War, on the 3rd September 1939. In 1943, she travelled to England. Because it was still wartime, this was not easy and communication was sometimes delayed. Indeed, there were problems getting out of wartime Grenada and Hilda Gibbs missed travelling with the group of other scholarship students leaving Trinidad on a similar mission. She remembers that this group of students, whose members she met later, represented different races. There was Stanley Fung, who was Chinese, Frank Williams, African, Bhagwan Singh, an Indian, and another, a Caribbean white, whose name she could not recall.

Hilda travelled by sloop to Trinidad. Of that trip, she recalled that her father was "lying outside the door, protecting his virgin daughter". From Trinidad, Hilda travelled with Basil Diaz, a young man from St Kitts, also going to study in England, who had travelled to Trinidad to get the plane. "Basil Diaz," she added, "was later a magistrate in Grenada." Also on that trip with her, part of the group that became friends, was a young GI bride travelling with her baby to meet her husband. From Trinidad, the group travelled on Pan American Airways (PANAM) through Santo Domingo to Miami, and from there by train to New York. They had an unplanned overnight stop in Santo Domingo because a hurricane threatened. Her memory of Santo Domingo included a meeting with an aged man who asked her why she was going to England, with all the dangers of war. She could not remember what she said to him, but explained when we spoke that her father had been focused not on war or its dangers but on sending her to study medicine.

Hilda Gibbs was then in her early twenties. She remembered a long walk to find a place to stay overnight in the Dominican Republic. In Miami, she was met by a representative of the British Consulate who had been sent to meet her and take her to the train for New York. The consular officer knew nothing about the friends who accompanied her, and would not assume responsibility for them, so Hilda decided not to leave those who had become her travelling companions. After the departure of the consular officer, Kittitian Basil Diaz took charge. He asked a taxi driver to take the group to a "nice, inexpensive hotel", but they didn't like the place to which the driver took them and decided to return to the train station. When they had deposited their luggage in a waiting room, Basil went for a walk. Hilda remembered that her father had asked her to send him a telegram when she got to Miami. Thinking that the young GI bride's husband would not know what time she would be arriving, Hilda offered to send a telegram to the young woman's husband. She recalled: "She bent forward to pay me, and I said, "Later". When Hilda had returned from sending the telegrams and the young woman opened her bag to pay, her train ticket and purse were gone. "The baby was restless," the GI bride explained, and a passing woman had advised her to walk the baby. That woman, they concluded, must have taken the money. Hilda Gibbs was faced with a dilemma. She explained to me, "I had money, my father's last penny that he had saved and taken from the bank to give me for a rainy day". Deciding that this was a good "rainy day", Hilda Gibbs bought the young woman a ticket to New York. "Between us," Dr Bynoe recalled, "we bought milk for the child and shared everything with her, including pillows that we rented on the train. We were eligible for three pillows. Two went to her and the baby. Basil and I shared one." She remembered conditions on the trip as "awful", with the smell of urine and water everywhere. This, she explained, was the "Jim Crow" era and they were given the compartments appropriate to their race.

She recalled being met in New York, and encountering relatives, one of them a La Touche, connected because one of Mayet's children, her grandmother Anne Redhead, had married a La Touche. Pleased to meet with relatives and members of a Caribbean diaspora[1] in the United States, Hilda seized the opportunity to make a plea for donations for sports equipment for St Joseph's Convent. She was developing an early awareness of the importance of family networks in the Caribbean diaspora whose remittances home were already, and have remained, so important to Caribbean economic survival and development. Welcoming her as a relative and a Grenadian, her New

York contacts also gave her "a beautiful fur-lined winter coat". She remembered that she "never felt the cold in New York" and that, before she left, she received a "beautiful letter" from the woman's G.I. husband, "with every cent of my money back". She concluded that story with a comment about the GI bride and her husband: "I always felt their children would be good citizens." Hilda's father had also written to Reggie Clyne, a Grenadian in the USA, "who played a big part in my life when I was going to England". Again, Dr Bynoe showed her awareness of the struggles that Caribbean people in the diaspora made in their attempts to share the perceived and actual benefits of United States' society with those at home and support new arrivals as they moved into or through American society. Reggie Clyne, to whom her father had written, was "highly educated but a railway porter in New York". When she met him, Reggie Clyne gave Hilda two books: Joel Augustus Roger's *From to Superman to Man* (1917) and *The Life of Toussaint L'Ouverture*. Rogers (1883-1966) was a Jamaican-born settler in the USA, whose self-published book was one of the earliest Black polemics to take apart the assumptions of racism. *The Life of Toussaint L'Ouverture* referred to may have been either J. R. Beard's *The Life of Toussaint L'Ouverture: The Negro Patriot of Hayti* (1853) or Ralph Korngold's *Citizen Toussaint* (New York: Little, Brown, 1944). The important point to note here is that Dame Hilda recalled that she was introduced to this type of literature in New York, and that, although she had read a lot in Grenada, she hadn't known of this kind of radical, race-conscious work.

Dr Bynoe recalled celebrating her twenty-second birthday, in November 1943, on the ship *USS Aquitaine*, going from New York to England. Although she was seriously pursuing her long-standing goal of embarking on a medical career, Hilda Gibbs was also a young woman who loved having a good time. Of her trip to England on the ship in wartime, she said: "There was a lot of wasting of time and playing bridge and having fun and… all this kind of thing." When I asked her if she had been anxious travelling in wartime, she said:

> "I will tell you a story and you will know that when you're young, death is not for you. You don't think of death as something that has anything to do with you."

USS Aquitaine was a troop ship taking American (United States) soldiers to England to fight in the Second World War. Dr Bynoe remembered meeting black American soldiers on board, and the mutual surprise and awkwardness of the young people as they encountered one another. They noted each other's existence but did not at first speak to each other. She recalled, too, the sound of sirens blowing shortly after they left harbour and the captain's warning that the sound of a siren was not one that should be ignored. When they heard the sound, he advised, they should grab lifejackets and proceed to the deck. This time it was a boat drill, the captain explained, but passengers should not let their guard down. The ship was not travelling under convoy and so was vulnerable. Dr Bynoe recreated the captain's tone and words from memory:

> "We are a fast ship and we're moving around. You will now be shown your lifeboat and the next time you hear a siren it may be a boat drill but you must not assume that. You must assume the worst."

The captain advised passengers that, since they were travelling in dangerous conditions, at night they should remove shoes "and hug your lifejacket when you get into bed. Any time you hear the siren," he warned, "get to your lifeboat". The young travellers, however, were not over-alarmed by these dire warnings of possible danger. Dr Bynoe recalled: "I used to take off my shoes, hug my lifejacket, get into bed and sleep like a top." Years later, she learnt that German U-boats had been moving throughout the North Atlantic. The young people from the Caribbean could not fail to be aware that a war was on, but they also enjoyed life and made adjustments with the characteristic resilience of youth. On board ship, Hilda developed a friendship with a group of Jewish women on their way to work with the United Nations Relief and Rehabilitation Administration (UNRRA).[2] The group was on its way to undertake relief work in a Europe battered by war. Some of that battering became evident to Hilda Gibbs when they arrived in Scotland. She reported how, after the journey across the Atlantic,[3] "we landed at a place called Gourock, in Scotland. It was a cold, bleak night. We were tired and hungry and we saw steam. In the cold, any little bit of heat creates a cloud, so we realised there was some food activity down there."

In Gourock, Hilda and her friends went to find some tea. What she now calls "the little joke" is that, when given black tea, she asked for milk and sugar. She recalled that everyone around looked up. "Madam," she was told, "we haven't seen milk and sugar for years."

She also remembered that, although she didn't drink the tea given to her, she kept her hands around the cup so that she could get its warmth.

"No milk and sugar?" I asked.

"No milk and sugar," Dr Hilda Bynoe agreed, looking into the distance.

The story suggests a young woman ready for hardships, but not perhaps, as is usual for the young and relatively privileged of any generation, unconcerned about accustomed comforts.

Dr Bynoe recalls that in Scotland she met a young man from Grenada whose family she had known. In time, she also met other Grenadians who were stationed in Europe, in the Canadian army, and various students of medicine, nursing and the social services. She recalled, though, that she was the only black person on the train to London. She spoke of meeting members of the Quakers, and of being taken to Friends House. "I don't remember details. I got in touch with the UNRRA people. The Quakers contacted the Colonial Office. I went to a hostel in Collingham Gardens."[4] There, she met Gweneth O'Reilly, a Kittitian who was in London to study medicine. For a long time, Hilda and Gweneth were the only two young women who were part of the group of friends studying in London. By her own account, Hilda was shy, but Gweneth was even shyer, and that made Hilda more confident. The young men who were part of the group became "like brothers".

She told me that in London in those days people often ignored falling bombs. This was not by choice. They would not hear the bombs until the actual explosion of their fall. "We could only pray." She recalled how a U-Bomb had fallen on the anatomy lab of the Royal Free Hospital Medical School about five minutes after the lab had been vacated.

Because her departure from Grenada had been delayed, Hilda arrived in London too late to enter medical school that year and spent some time "at a polytechnic, taking classes in science" while she waited to enter medical school. During that year, while she awaited placement exams, she lived first at Collingham Gardens and then moved, with Gweneth, to an apartment in St John's Wood, near Swiss Cottage underground station. Frank and Stanley, young students from Guyana who had travelled earlier to London and were now a year ahead of Hilda, visited from time to time. Eventually, after the placement exam, Hilda got into London University and Gweneth, who later became godmother to Hilda's son Roland, entered university in Belfast. After Gweneth had left, she said, "the boys didn't think it was appropriate to come to see me alone." Of her time in England Dr Bynoe gave a succinct summary: "I went to England and I did my medicine, got married, had two children, came home."

"I did my medicine, got married..."

Peter Bynoe, like Hilda, legally a British colonial subject, was from Trinidad and in the Royal Air Force (R.A.F.). True Caribbean colonials, the two met at a cricket match at Lord's Cricket ground in London. Again, the narrative helps to shed light on the social interactions of the period and the place. After attending a funeral, Hilda and Marjorie Valere, whose future husband, Kester McMillan was to become a notable figure in the legal profession of Trinidad & Tobago, decided to go to a cricket match at Lords where Learie Constantine, famed Trinidadian all-rounder, was captaining a Commonwealth cricket team against England. Dame Hilda recalled, "As we came in, I heard this shout, and Marjorie looked around and she said, "Peter Bynoe!" The friendship with Marjorie Valere was to last a long time and to be shared by other members of the family through the generations. With Peter Bynoe it was not "love at first sight." A week after the meeting at Lord's cricket ground, they met again at a party in Collingham Gardens. Dame Hilda recalled:

> "We are dancing, the music stops, his partner moves away, so does mine. He says, "You don't remember me, do you?" I said no. He said, "Marjorie Valere introduced us." I thought, "So what?"

Because of the gender imbalance among Caribbean students in London at that time, socially "women ruled the roost". Hilda Gibbs told Peter that she would love to dance with him, but later. Later, she encountered him again with his friend Gavin Scott, who intervened on Peter's behalf. "So I hear you wouldn't dance with my friend. How could you do that?" Dr Bynoe then told me, "So I danced with him, and didn't stop dancing." She had already been dating, and did not at first acknowledge any particular attraction to the R.A.F. officer, but this soon changed.

Through all these experiences, Hilda was working hard, anxious about her studies. Her explanations provide some insight into the migrant students' perceptions of themselves and of their relationship with the host community, the "mother country". She said, "If you failed your first year, you would be sent back home, because their own people were coming out of the army and they wanted places for them."

As a young student, Hilda Gibbs felt both the effects of gender discrimination and the immediate wartime pressures on colonial students because they were taking up coveted positions that could be filled by British ex-soldiers who were looking for places in educational and other institutions at the end of a war. Foreign medical students had to prove that they merited the university places afforded them. "I worked hard but I remember I got married at the end of the first year [of medical school].[5] Friends had to lend us ration coupons for a wedding dress. The suit Peter had been given when he left the RAF was smart enough for the wedding." In Grenada, her father and the rest of the family were not enthusiastic about the idea of a marriage before Hilda was finished with medical school, but they left the decision to her. Eventually, when he met Peter Bynoe, Joseph Gibbs approved his daughter's choice. But there were no parents at the wedding. Both mothers had already died and for the fathers travelling was difficult and expensive, and neither was wealthy. Dr Bynoe said that at this period, she learned how supportive her new husband could be. "Peter was in the background and he was very good about it all."

Hilda and Peter Bynoe were married on September 3rd, 1947, after she had passed her first MB, roughly four years after her arrival in England. She went on to qualify in 1951, the same year that her father, in Grenada, was elected to the legislature under the banner of Eric Gairy's People's Party. The Bynoes' first son, Roland, was born in 1952 and Michael (Mickey), in 1953. The family returned to Grenada in December 1953. Somewhere amidst those intense years of medical school, marriage, babies, and trying to manage their finances for life in London, the couple found time for a WISU (the newly formed West Indian Students' Union) trip to Yugoslavia.

Hilda Gibbs and Peter Bynoe, 1947

The West Indian Students' Union

As the historians tell it, the formation of the West Indian Students' Union in England was a direct result of inter and post-war migration and student perception that they needed an organisation that would be concerned with their socio-political needs. David Clover, of University of London's Institute of Commonwealth Studies, writes:

> The West Indian Students' Union was formed in 1945 with the expansion in the number of students arriving in London and elsewhere for further and higher education, and acted as a welfare, political and social organisation. Many future leaders of Caribbean states and territories would occupy positions of leadership within the West Indian Students' Union.[6]

The post World War II population of Caribbean students in London reflected the rise in Caribbean presence generally. According to Clover:

> Before World War Two at no time did the number of colonial students at universities rise as high as 2000 in a single year. After the war, the number of overseas students of all origins rose year by year and by 1960-61 there were 35,729 British students from the Commonwealth and United Kingdom dependencies at universities and other institutions of higher learning and of these 6949 were from the British Caribbean.[7]

Clover reports that "in 1939 there had been 166 West Indian students in Britain, by 1947 there were 929, and three years later (by 1950) there were 1114.

As Dame Hilda told it, she and her friend Jean Oppenheim were the initiators of the organisation that became the West Indian Students' Union. Like many other students who studied in various parts of Britain, Jean Oppenheim visited London and stayed at the hostel at 18 Collingham Gardens. The hostels at 18 and later also 16 Collingham Gardens became a centre for gatherings of West Indian students. Both Gibbs and Oppenheim were interested in the idea of having a union of students, and they eventually called a meeting. Interested students attended and the group elected officers to carry the idea forward. Dr Bynoe recalled that many Jamaicans were involved. Jean Oppenheim was a member of the committee that emerged from those initial meetings, but Hilda Bynoe, newly married and a medical student, didn't think she could find the time to carry out the duties of a committee member. As a student of architecture, Peter Bynoe was also a member of WISU.

Dr Bynoe recalled political struggles in the early days of WISU'S existence. "A left wing," she commented, "almost planned a coup", but there were enough like-minded people to keep it the kind of organisation they wanted it to be. In its early days, WISU arranged hostel accommodation for students visiting London; acted as a point of contact for Caribbean intellectuals visiting England; and invited "eminent people" visiting from the Caribbean to speak to them. When President Josip Tito's Yugoslavia needed people to help build a railway, the students of WISU, including the then WISU president Forbes Burnham, made a trip to Yugoslavia to spend time building the railway.

Dr Bynoe's account bears out Clover's claim that these West Indian students "attended universities, the inns of Court, polytechnics and technical colleges, and teaching hospitals." Clover's account also suggests that Hilda Gibbs was one of an increasing number of women students who, given opportunities for scholarships to acquire further education, were entering educational institutions in England. However, one of the concerns of WISU, she explained, was to discuss the terms and conditions under which a University of the West Indies would come into being.[8]

Within the ranks of WISU, Hilda Bynoe met others who were to become West Indian leaders and political thinkers. Guyana's Forbes Burnham (later Guyana's prime minister and then president) was an early WISU president.[9] Trinidadian Geraldine Connor, later a theatre director, ethnomusicologist and Professor at Leeds University, was a Vice-Chairman of WISU in the 1940s.[10] Arthur Lewis from St Lucia, an economist, was later a Nobel Prize winner. Derek Knight, Peter Bynoe's roommate, was to become Minister of Legal Affairs in the government of Grenada's Premier (and subsequently Prime Minister) Eric Gairy. WISU was a place where future West Indian leaders could meet and discuss the situation of West Indians in London, at home in the Caribbean and worldwide.

Like other students in London, the Bynoes made many new friendships which were to be important later in their personal and political lives. London also served as a launching pad for visits to other places in Europe. In addition to travelling with the West Indian Students' Union to do community work in Yugoslavia, the Bynoes visited Zarnen, Switzerland, beginning associations that were to last a lifetime and to become part of the friendships later treasured by their sons.

Pan-African Influences

Dr Bynoe recalled that in England she went to meetings of Harold Moody's Pan-Africanist organisation.[11] She recalled being influenced by George Padmore,[12] W.E.B. DuBois[13] and the Pan African Congress. Her reference to these African diaspora intellectuals indicates how much, as a student in London, Hilda Bynoe was part of the general ferment of interest in Africa at home and abroad. This was a time when C.L.R. James, George Padmore and others were active in London, and in 1945, the Manchester Pan African Conference was attended by black leaders Jomo Kenyatta, Kwame Nkrumah and W.E.B. DuBois.

From the influences of her youth, and her understanding of the struggles of her ancestors, she already valued the contributions of the Amerindian Mayet and of people like her paternal grandmother, the Dominican Yoruba woman, Ma Sese. Now, as she encountered intellectual activists in London, she was developing a more analytical framework for her interest in Africa and the African contribution to the Caribbean.

The previous chapter noted that whilst Hilda Gibbs was working as a teacher in San Fernando, Trinidad, she had been exposed to the influence of her cousin David Pitt, and his mother, and with Pitt, Gomes, Patrick Solomon and others, she had been a member of Trinidad's West Indian National Party (WINP). In fact, a closer look at the story of David Pitt provides some context not only for her pan-Africanist ideas but also for her ambition and sense of herself.

Born in Grenada on October 3, 1913, David Pitt was influenced by T.A. Marryshow and the idea that *The West Indies must be West Indian,* the motto of Marryshow's newspaper. In 1932, having studied at the Grenada Boys' Secondary School, Pitt "won Grenada's only overseas scholarship to attend the prestigious medical school at the University of Edinburgh in Scotland".[14] Between 1938 and 1947, he practised in St Vincent and Trinidad. According to his own account, he had returned to the Caribbean because of the pull of Caribbean politics and society. "I turned down a lucrative post in Ghana because the pull of Caribbean politics proved too irresistible for a newly qualified, politically active doctor."[14] As a founding member and president of the West Indian National Party, he lobbied the British Government for independence for Trinidad as part of a West Indies federation, a radical idea in those days. *The New Leader*, a paper edited by the British Labour politician and anti-imperialist Fenner Brockway, and the ideas of Trinidadian political activist and pan-Africanist George Padmore were also amongst Pitt's influences. Settling in London in 1947, he was active in black British politics throughout the 1950s, confronting issues of racial prejudice and other forms of discrimination. With the encouragement of Martin Luther King, Jr., he started an organisation to campaign against racial discrimination, CARD (Campaign Against Racial Discrimination), of which he became Chair in 1965. In 1975, he was appointed to the House of Lords by Prime Minister Harold Wilson and became Lord Pitt of Hampstead.[15]

When Dame Hilda was made Governor of Grenada, and visited London for her 1969 investiture as a Dame Commander of the British Empire, David Pitt was by that time Deputy Chairman of the Greater London Council (GLC). Another relative, Baroness Ros Howells,[16] who had grown up with her as a sister, was active in Black politics for many years, and was made a life peer by the Tony Blair Labour government in 1999. All of this had an influence on the ideas and attitudes of Hilda Gibbs Bynoe. Or perhaps, more accurately, all of this shows that Hilda Gibbs Bynoe was part of a family involved in political activism.

Triumphs and Disappointments

Looking back, although she was pleased with the achievements of her personal and professional life, Dr Bynoe was conscious that there were also disappointments. She told me:

> "My aspirations professionally were not satisfied. I wanted to specialise in surgery to begin with, or gynaecology. I should have had my first job at the Elizabeth Garrett Anderson hospital.[17] They offered me a place in obstetrics, and I was lying in a hospital bed with a threatened miscarriage. So I come home as a qualified doctor with two babies and we go to Grenada and – now remember I'm a scholarship winner – I have to go back home. Peter goes with me. He's an architect, and they don't know what an architect is in Grenada. They offer him a job as an engineer and he has no training in engineering."

Dr Bynoe's story highlights the early struggles of young professionals trying to find a footing in their colonial societies after qualifying in
their chosen fields. Both the Bynoes were anxious to find jobs
commensurate with their qualifications and also to find some degree
of job satisfaction. Colonial students in receipt of scholarships were
required to return to their countries to serve. This could, Dr Bynoe
explained, mean anywhere in the Caribbean, in the islands (and other
lands) that were colonies of Britain. However, she was now married,
and as a woman she was expected to follow her husband and could do
so without penalty, as long as the couple lived in one of the colonies.
When there was no job for Peter Bynoe in Grenada, the two returned
to Trinidad. Later, still seeking the best place in which to develop their
careers, the Bynoes travelled to Guyana and then back to Trinidad.
Like her husband, Hilda Bynoe was ready to work at her chosen
profession, but she was also a wife and mother, and gender expectations were to play a role in the shaping of her life in the Caribbean.

Endnotes

1. For more comments on the impact of diaspora, see Chapter
   Two, pp. 37-43
2. Established in 1943, UNRRA was the administrative body
   (1943–47) for an extensive social-welfare programme that assisted
   nations ravaged by World War II. Created on Nov. 9, 1943,
   by a 44-nation agreement, its operations concentrated on
   distributing relief supplies, such as food, clothing, fuel, shelter,
   and medicines; providing relief services, with trained personnel;
   and aiding agricultural and economic rehabilitation. In addition,
   it also provided camps, personnel, and food for the care and
   repatriation of millions of displaced persons and refugees after
   the war. UNRRA discontinued its activities in 1947. See the
   Encyclopaedia Britannica – http://www.britannica.com/
   EBchecked/topic/616468/United-Nations-Relief-and-
   Rehabilitation-Administration).
3. My search for records of ships transporting soldiers to Europe
   during wartime yielded the following comment at <http://
   www.ww2troopships.com/crossings/1942b.htm>: "The records
   of ships used to carry troops to their theaters of operations

were destroyed intentionally in 1951 [...] According to our [U. S. National Archives] records, in 1951 the Department of the Army destroyed all passenger lists, manifests, logs of vessels, and troop movement files of United States Army Transports for World War II." (There was no word on why the records were destroyed.) Thus there is no longer an official record of who sailed on what ship, though there are still valuable sources that can be found. So this web page is an informal collecting ground for information about troopship crossings."

4. 1a Collingham Gardens was later the address of the Embassy of Grenada in London.

5. Hilda and Peter Bynoe married in 1947. Since Mrs. Bynoe remembers celebrating her twenty-second birthday (November 18, 1943, on the ship), she is likely to have arrived in London, England at the end of 1943 or early in 1944. She recalls being too late for university entry, presumably in January, and having to take courses while she waited for the following year. The timeline suggests that, after a preliminary year of studies at a London polytechnic, she began her studies at London University in 1945.

6. See "The Society for Caribbean Studies Annual Conference Papers", Volume 6, 2005, Edited Sandra Courtman. See http://www.caribbeanstudies.org.uk/papers/2005/olvol6p10.PDF. See also, David Clover, "Dispersed or Destroyed: Archives, The West Indian Students' Union and Public Memory".

7. David Clover, "Dispersed or Destroyed".

8. Established in 1945, the then University College of the West Indies was at first at College of the University of London.

9. Premier of Guyana 1964-66, Prime Minister 1966-80, President 1980-85.

10. After a long and distinguished career, Geraldine Connor died in the U.K. in October 2011.

11. Harold Moody (1882-1947) was a Jamaican-born doctor who practised in London. He formed the League of Coloured Peoples in 1931.

12. George Padmore (1903-1959) a Trinidadian, birth name Malcolm Nurse, was initially a communist activist in the USA, then went to the USSR working for the Comintern until he broke from it over its failure to support colonial freedom. Barred

from re-entry to the USA, he settled in London. Sharply critical
of Stalinism, though still a revolutionary socialist, he was a
trusted aide of Kwame Nkrumah.

13. W.E.B. Du Bois (1868-1963) was an African American sociologist,
historian, activist and leading figure in the Pan Africanist
movement. His *The Souls of Black Folk* (1903) was probably
the single most important document of black consciousness
for the first half of the twentieth century.

14. "Travellers' Guide, Grenada. http://www.travelgrenada.com/
Lord_Pitt.html.

15. Roy Francis and Juliette Foster, "Lord Pitt The Gentle
Statesman." *The New York Christian News*, p. 4.

16. Ros Howells (1931-): Rosalind Patricia-Anne Howells was
born in Grenada. For her work in race and community relations
in London she was made a Labour peer, Baroness Howells
of St David's (her parish in Grenada), in 1999.

17. A hospital in London, U.K.

CHAPTER FIVE
RETURN TO THE CARIBBEAN AND THE ROAD TO GOVERNORSHIP

As two young professionals returning to the colonial Caribbean after years of professional training, Hilda and Peter Bynoe encountered problems trying to find appropriate jobs. They wanted to make a contribution to their small island economies, but to do so they had to gain respect from the colonial bureaucracy, and accommodate themselves to gender responsibilities and expectations. Dr Bynoe was offered a WHO scholarship to study Public Health. She declined, deciding that this would be difficult with her responsibilities for her young children and family. Her personal experience of the problems for a young professional who was also a wife and mother confirm the argument of Caribbean sociologist, Eudine Barriteau, who writes that "an understanding of the social relations of gender and gender systems should be pivotal to any assessment and critiquing of Caribbean societies".[1] Both gender and race relations in a colonial polity are critical to understanding the post-qualification experiences of Dr Bynoe. In Trinidad, she secured a job in the maternity ward of the Port of Spain hospital. Her husband, meanwhile, was finding it difficult to secure a job that suited his qualifications, or even be given the recognition and salary that would be commensurate with his qualifications. He could find a job, but not at the salary level that would be given to his white peers. Confronted with what both he and his wife considered discriminatory attitudes on the part of the colonial government, Peter Bynoe refused to take the job he was offered. As a qualified architect, with the RIBA (Associate of the Royal Institute of British Architects) qualification, he felt he should be treated as any other person with similar qualifications. In the mid nineteen-fifties, as a young black couple, rejecting discrimination, and with a sense of themselves that made them deeply resentful of what they considered colonial condescension, the Bynoes began looking for positions that would accord them the respect and recognition they felt they had earned. It was not an easy task but the young couple had the confidence to insist on being accorded respect. In Hilda Bynoe's family, there were others of her generation also struggling to establish professional reputations, and Peter Bynoe was not the first generation of his family to become professionally qualified. A maternal uncle had studied medicine in Glasgow, and in Peter Bynoe's generation, a younger brother had also been in the British air force during World War Two, and had studied medicine. Even so, for the family of Peter and Hilda Bynoe, with two young children and at first only Dr Bynoe working, it was difficult to manage.

The Bynoes were ready to take a job anywhere in the world. "We tried Africa and we tried everywhere, and we got this job in Guyana." This account seems not unlike that of others graduating from colleges and universities then and now in the Caribbean. Graduates who are not from developed countries that are more able to absorb them have to be willing to spread their nets further afield, and be prepared to take a job anywhere one might be offered. For the Bynoes, there was the difficulty of satisfying the personal and professional needs of both partners, because they worked in different professional fields. Indeed, in Grenada, Peter Bynoe, a qualified architect, was offered a job as an engineer in the Public Works Department. There were gender issues, too, for Hilda Bynoe, as she looked to practice her profession.

After a few weeks at home in Crochu, St Andrew's, Grenada, the couple went with their "two babies", Roland and Mickey (Michael), to Trinidad. One of the attractions was that, in colonial Trinidad, there appeared, said Dr Bynoe, to have been "no discriminatory laws against women doctors at that time". She became part of the Trinidad Civil Service, working as a public health doctor. She worked at the treatment of illnesses such as yaws, venereal disease and tuberculosis. Part of a team of doctors, nurses and male health workers, she went to clubs along the Wrightson Road area, examined club hostesses, and brought them back to base for treatment if they were infected. She also went out to rural areas to work in clinics. She recalled being offered a bribe by a man who worked in the oilfields. Workers were sometimes sent by their bosses to be tested. If infected, they were suspended until free of infection, thus losing income. In one particular case, when the man returned the following week, he carried an envelope of money which he offered to Dr Bynoe. Her colleagues laughed when she told them about it. It was, it seemed, a known pattern. Dr Bynoe recalled a professional connection with Grenada during this year of work in Trinidad. The Chief Doctor at the Public Health Centre in Trinidad was a Grenadian, Dr Gordon Gentle.

After one year's employment in Trinidad, the Bynoes went to Guyana. There, they discovered that colonial Guyana was not giving full-time jobs to women doctors and that it was generally difficult to find employment for professional women. Dr Bynoe was offered a three-year contract, which she described as having "discriminatory clauses".

The Bynoes worked for some years in Guyana, and then, following the needs of Peter's career, returned to Trinidad. There, Dr Bynoe could not at first find a full-time job, because, it seemed to her, the employment conditions in colonial Trinidad appeared to have become as discriminatory as those in Guyana and she would have to work under a short-term contract. As one assesses Dr Bynoe's experiences at this juncture, it is clear that the colonial political system discriminated against the specific needs of women.

Still seeking to assert her civic relevance in the face of an obstructive system, Dr Bynoe eventually secured employment as District Medical Officer in what was then the village of Diego Martin, Trinidad. (It is now a middle-income outer suburb of Port of Spain.) Often this job felt onerous. On the one hand, she felt conscious that the public considered her a person of privilege, while on the other she felt oppressed by overwork and the small financial returns. So, as she told me, "And then one day I gave it up. It was intensive, tiring work. And then came that day."

On the day Dr Bynoe decided to give up her practice, she had seen a good many patients and was exhausted. She decided to stop work for the day, much to the displeasure of some, and in particular one woman, who had been waiting for a long time. The woman expressed her opinion that since Dr Bynoe was a government employee, she was obliged to give attendance. Dr Bynoe, insisting that she could see no more patients that day and aware that she had already done much more than required under her government contract, wrote a letter referring the woman's child to the hospital clinic. Then she wrote another letter – her own letter of resignation from the government

Dr Hilda Bynoe, circa 1969

service – and proceeded to enter private practice. In private practice, she felt she could offer the kind of service she wished to give. Her private practice began in 1965.

Of her politics during those days in Trinidad, Dr Bynoe says, "I was a strong PNM (People's National Movement)[2] woman... I was a member of the PNM." Peter Bynoe, on the other hand, did not become a member of any political organisation. As a member of the PNM women's group, Dr Bynoe became friends with Muriel Donawa McDavidson,[4] a Minister in the PNM government, and their friendship provided both women with an opportunity to do the kind of work that was important to them and "be of service to others". "Muriel," Doctor Bynoe declared, "... was in a Ministry where she was in a position to help the poor, and Muriel and I became friends because the practice that I was building up in St James came from... those same people that I used to work with in the Government offices..."

An unofficial social welfare agreement developed between the village doctor and the Minister of Social Affairs, both concerned to improve the conditions of the working people of their country. Indicating her attitude towards education and the social services in this period, Dr Bynoe said, "I always taught. All my life as a doctor I taught." She always saw her profession as an opportunity to teach the working poor about health.

1967 and after: Towards the Governorship

These details of Dr Bynoe's career after qualifying and returning to Trinidad begin to map the route toward the governorship of Grenada. Dr Bynoe's father, Joseph Gibbs, visited one day from Grenada and informed the Bynoes that Grenada's Premier, Eric Gairy, wanted her to be Grenada's Governor. A member of Gairy's political team since he first contested elections in 1951, Hilda's father was by then a senior member of the administration. Several people attest to Eric Gairy's respectful attitude toward Uncle Joe, the attitude of a younger man toward an older one whose example and advice he valued. Dr Bynoe commented that there was a father-son relationship between the two, that the father might not always have agreed with the son, but that he never deserted him.

By 1967, Dr Bynoe's professional life had not yielded all that she had hoped it would. She had a thriving private practice, but her roles as wife and mother had prevented her from concentrating on professional advancement and doing the kind of specialisation she would have liked. She had applied to pursue a course in psychiatry at the Mona, Jamaica campus of the University of the West Indies, but the message from Grenada came before she received a response from the University of the West Indies to her application.

In 1967, Grenada and other Eastern Caribbean islands became Associated States of Britain, which meant that they now had control over all internal affairs, while the British government retained responsibility for external affairs and defence. This moved the islands constitutionally closer to independent status. Premier Gairy's initial choice as Governor of the new Associated State was T. Joseph Gibbs, but when asked to be Governor, Joseph Gibbs did not accept the post but suggested that his daughter might accept if asked. Dr Bynoe explained: "It was my father's suggestion, and Gairy liked the idea."

Considering her options, Dr Bynoe reviewed the trajectory of her career. The year she qualified, the University of the West Indies (UWI) had been offering jobs to junior people. Because she was a woman with a family and young children, she hadn't been able to take up that opportunity. Continually throughout that early period of her professional life, it seemed to her that gender discrimination and family considerations had intervened to narrow her choices. With a young family, she could not consider further specialisation and the kind of postgraduate work she would have enjoyed. She did, though, take opportunities to update her qualifications. In 1964, she spent from September to December in England, taking courses in obstetrics & gynaecology from the University of London British Postgraduate Medical Federation. She took the opportunity because her husband, pursuing his own professional interests, was going to be in India for one year.

She also had an interest in psychiatry, and was trying to pursue that quietly, writing to her friend Dr Michael Beaubrun in Jamaica, testing the waters, finding out what opportunities were available and trying to determine how she might pursue her ambitions with two young children as part of the equation. In the event, Dr Beaubrun was away when she wrote. Unaware of this, Dr Bynoe waited, still wondering how to balance her commitments and desire to advance professionally. It was while she awaited Dr Beaubrun's response that her father visited her to inform of Eric Gairy's proposal. She reflected that she had always been interested in the possibilities of postcolonial politics. She was ready to take an imaginative leap into a completely different way of life.

"I was conscious of the fact that I was equal to all and superior to many who were ahead of me," she said, but there were other factors and individuals helping Dr Bynoe to make the decision. She decided to speak to Audrey Jeffers, a veteran of women's struggle in Trinidad, whom she described as "one of the people (who) had a lot of influence on my generation of women."

Born in an upper middle-class family, Audrey Jeffers (1898-1968) arrived in England in 1913 to study Social Science. During the 1914-18 war, she worked among the West African troops in Britain and organised a West African soldiers' fund. *The Encyclopaedia of Women Social Reformers* also credits Ms Jeffers with being involved in founding, while in London, the Union of Students of African Descent, which was a precursor of the League of Coloured Peoples.[6] She returned to Trinidad in 1920 where she opened a school for the poor at her parents' home, and did social work among the poorer classes. In the 1920s, she established the Coterie of Social workers to improve local conditions. This group was responsible for providing free school lunches for poor children and establishing breakfast sheds to help the poor.[5] She was the first woman elected to the Port-of-Spain City Council in 1936, and the first female member of the Legislative Council of Trinidad & Tobago in 1946.

When Dr Bynoe and her husband went to see "aunt" Audrey Jeffers, she at first dismissed the idea because she hadn't realised that the offer of a governorship was to Dr Bynoe. She thought that Peter Bynoe was the one being offered the post and she couldn't fathom why he would want to give up a promising post in Trinidad to go to Grenada as governor at a point of his career when he was advancing in his field. However, when Audrey Jeffers realised the offer was for Dr Bynoe, she responded with enthusiasm. Audrey Jeffers, Dr Bynoe explained, knew that as a man Peter Bynoe had – and would have – many opportunities for professional advancement as an architect. On the other hand, the position as first woman governor in the British commonwealth of nations would be important not only to Hilda Bynoe personally, but to Caribbean women generally. Ms Jeffers, a woman dedicated to the idea of community service and the advancement of women, gave both support and encouragement, helping Dr Bynoe toward a decision she had already half made.

Meanwhile, the British authorities had been aware that with the 1967 constitutional changes, and the new designation of Associated Statehood, Eric Gairy would be able to choose his own governor. Sir Ian Turbott, the British governor then in office, was known to want a little time before a new appointee would take his place. According to Dr Bynoe, "He really wanted to stay in Grenada another year."

The Bynoes went to Grenada to meet with Eric Gairy, who formally invited Hilda Bynoe to be governor. From that first interview, Dr Bynoe asserted her independence, stopping Eric Gairy mid-sentence when he tried to talk about his personal reputation and how onlookers might view his invitation to her to be governor. "Your personal reputation," she advised him, "has nothing whatever to do with Hilda and Peter Bynoe." She was able to maintain her independence through various difficult situations in Grenada during the period of her governorship, Dr Bynoe considered, because she had asserted it from the beginning. Although Dr Bynoe did not elaborate, the reference to Eric Gairy's "personal reputation" and her anxiety to distance herself from any commentary on this, was probably a pointed way of putting distance between herself and the less salubrious aspects of Eric Gairy's vaunted reputation with women. As Gordon Rohlehr has noted: "[the] popular mind had learnt to associate the vain things of the flesh" less with leaders like Trinidad's Eric Williams and "more with leaders such as... Eric Gairy of Grenada".[7]

Dr Bynoe was giving early warning that she would not allow herself to become a part of commentary – or sly conversation – about Eric Gairy's private life. Other comments made by Dr Bynoe about her period as governor suggest that Eric Gairy did not enjoy this independent aspect of her approach. According to Dr Bynoe, Eric Gairy had "his people" guarding Government House while she occupied it as governor. The reference to "his people" might be interpreted as relating to the paramilitary group that came to be known in Grenada as the "Mongoose gang", a group that had the reputation for sometimes violently enforcing loyalty to Gairy.

In Grenada, both Hilda and Peter Bynoe had to find their path through various alliances and overtures of friendship. Both Bynoes had prior friendships with people in Grenada. Now, such friendships could be interpreted as evidence of cooperation with one political party or the other. The Hon. Derek Knight, who was a member of Eric Gairy's cabinet, and an important part of his political team, had been Peter Bynoe's flatmate when they were students together in London. The Bynoes decided that they would have to be careful, though Derek Knight was a long-standing friend, as were other members of his family. They had also developed a friendship with Mr George Hosten, another member of the Gairy cabinet.

Trinidad said goodbye to Dr Bynoe with style. Events impresario Aubrey Adams, at the time rapidly becoming a cultural icon and subsequently cultural advisor to Prime Minister Eric Williams, was asked to prepare a show at the Port of Spain Savannah, usual venue for major cultural events. Invited to this gala, the public filled the Savannah. Dr Bynoe recalled that "When we arrived, I was ushered into a seat next to Dr Williams." Although a member of Dr Williams's People's National Party (PNM), Hilda Bynoe had not been happy with Dr Williams' handling of matters surrounding the end of the 1958 attempt at a Federation of the West Indies. She explained that "after the Federation, the rest of the Caribbean wanted Dr Williams to take on the premiership, or Prime-Ministership". Like her Grenadian-born but Trinidadian settled compatriot, the calypsonian Mighty Sparrow (Slinger Francisco)[8], Dr Bynoe recalled what she referred to as "the famous bit of mathematics" by Dr Williams: One from ten leaves nought. In 1962, Jamaica had opted out of the Federation. Williams (and therefore Trinidad) decided he would not continue to try to make it work. A federal future was not deemed a high enough priority to make what may have been considered a local (Trinidad national) sacrifice. Dr Bynoe had "never forgiven Dr Williams that bit of mathematics." It must have seemed a hypocritical bit of back-tracking on commitments she had heard Williams give. She recalled that when the Federation first started, the rest of the Caribbean had been anxious to have Guyana included as one of its number. While the Bynoes lived in Guyana, Dr Williams had visited, she said, "and made a famous speech, and I heard him say that any federation of the West Indies would be better than no federation." In her estimation, Dr Williams could, if he had wanted to, have made a difference to the story of Caribbean integration. Her assessment when we talked was that perhaps Dr Williams knew his constituency and was conscious that the Indians (in Trinidad) would have been hesitant about supporting a federation that would unequivocally mark them as a racial minority. In spite of her recognition of Dr Williams' dilemma, there was still bitterness at the memory of his decision when we spoke.

In 1968, as Governor-designate of Grenada, Dr Bynoe met Dr Williams personally for the first time. The moment came when Dr Williams rose and bowed in acknowledgement of the Governor-designate. Dr Bynoe rose, and together the two stepped forward to the microphone. In his address, Dr Williams celebrated the appointment and expressed pleasure at Trinidad's sending one of its children to Grenada. After Dr Williams's address, Dr Bynoe gave a brief acknowledgement of the honour and the event was over.

The Trinidad Guardian was vocal about what this appointment would mean for women. "Trinidad women rejoice", it announced, and a subheading suggested that "Appointment seen as a Challenge to Fairer sex".[9] *The Trinidad Guardian* also showed a pipe-smoking, bearded Peter Bynoe alongside the announcement that "Governor's Husband to quit Trinidad Post". The story read: "The Trinidad Government is to lose its Chief Architect, Mr Peter Bynoe, who said yesterday that he would be giving up his job here to accompany his wife for her tour of duty as Governor of Grenada." Commenting obliquely on this unique gender dynamic, the paper noted that "Up to yesterday, Mr Bynoe, who admitted that he had suddenly found himself "a man in an exclusive position", could not say what his role as the husband of "the first woman Governor ever in the Commonwealth would be like." According to the newspaper, Peter Bynoe anticipated that he would have to become involved in several activities at his wife's side. The newspaper quoted him as saying, "Time and protocol will tell... I will have to play it by ear."

The Bynoes travelled to Grenada by yacht and were given a rapturous welcome. When they made the journey, their son Roland, who was sixteen, was at high school in Barbados. Mickey, the younger at fifteen, was at St Mary's College, Port-of-Spain, Trinidad. Later, both boys were awarded scholarships to continue their high school education at Williston Academy, Massachusetts, USA.

Endnotes

1. Violet Eudine Barriteau, "Confronting Power and Politics: A Feminist Theorizing of Gender in Commonwealth Caribbean Societies", *Meridians.* Volume 3. No. 2 (2003), p. 57.
2. Eudine Barriteau, "Confronting Power and Politics", p. 58
3. The People's National Movement, led by Dr Eric Williams, was formed in 1955. The party had a strong nationalist platform and led Trinidad & Tobago into independence in 1962.
4. Muriel Donawa McDavidson passed away in 2001, aged 72. She was an active figure in Trinidad political life for a number of years and a foundation member of the PNM.
5. See *The Trinidad Guardian,* August 1ˢᵗ, 1998, p. 41, <http:// www.nalis.gov.tt/Biography/AudreyJeffers.html>.
6. Helen Rappaport, *Encyclopedia of Women Social Reformers*, Volume 1. ABC-CLIO, 2001. See also Veronica Marie Gregg, *Caribbean Women: an anthology of non-fiction writing, 1890-1980, Volume 1.* (Indiana: University of Notre Dame Press, 2005).
7. Gordon Rohlehr, "The Culture of Williams: Culture, Performance, Legacy", *Callaloo,* Volume 20, No. 4, p. 855.
8. Calypsonian The Mighty Sparrow sang about the demise of the Federation, citing not only Jamaica's decision to opt out of the grouping but also the decision of Trinidad's Dr Eric Williams to pull out following Jamaica's departure, since "one from ten leaves nought". Sparrow's calypso was called "Federation".
9. *The Trinidad Guardian*, May 18, 1968.

CHAPTER SIX
DAME HILDA BYNOE, GOVERNOR OF GRENADA

In her creative writing collection, *I Woke at Dawn* (1996), Dame Hilda has a story entitled, "We never knew St George's". It tells the story of a rural child for whom the town, St George's, was a distant, unknown quantity. Government House, located at the top of Lucas Street, was the beginning of the area that the average person thought of as downtown St. George's, or, more familiarly, "town". In the story, Dame Hilda wrote:

> "We never knew St George's. We never saw its beauty from Fort Frederick, from Richmond Hill, Morne Jaloux or the hills of Jean Anglais.
> We never knew Silver Sands. We never heard the gentle music of its lapping waters nor the rumbling of breaking waves in Levera Bay.
> We never saw St George's from Grand Anse. We never saw it nestling on the hills and in the Valley below Fort St George. It was only a place, just a little market-town with streets and shops, and with people buying and selling things there, especially on Saturdays. Saturday was market day."[1]

For the young Hilda travelling to town from Crochu, Government House was "merely the beginning of town". Once near Government House, the beauty of Grenada, with the sea in the distance – something of the view that those coming into the country by sea would have – opened up before the rural traveller. To those from the countryside who didn't "know St George's", it was a distant beauty. But in spite of the admiration that Government House and the urban environment inspired, the young Hilda Bynoe was not overawed; she could see beyond the external beauty because of the wealth of connections she had with the land through Great Grandmother Mayet and her other relatives.

Of the beginning of her governorship Dr Bynoe explained that she had ensured she "was in Grenada when the announcement was made. They told me it was coming up and they asked me to come over." She left Trinidad and was at her family home in Crochu when the news was announced in the media.

The Trinidad & Tobago press had given Dr Bynoe a send-off fitting for a daughter of the soil going to take up an important post in a neighbouring country. The *Trinidad Guardian* of June 7, 1968, announced that Dr Bynoe, her husband, Peter, and son, Michael, had on the previous day waved goodbye to Trinidad from the deck of the *HTMS Courland Bay*, the ship that was taking them to Grenada from Chaguaramas, Trinidad. They were accompanied by the Permanent Secretary in the Ministry of Home Affairs and his Senior Assistant Secretary. When they arrived in Grenada on the *Courland Bay*, they were accompanied into Grenada's beautiful harbour by "a flotilla of small craft".[2]

The send-off from Trinidad and the welcome to Grenada, ninety miles away, were both moving. The *Trinidad Guardian* reported:

> As Dr Bynoe, accompanied by her husband Peter Bynoe and young son, Michael, stepped on Grenada soil, some 500 helium-filled balloons in the State's colours – green, yellow and blue – were sent aloft by pupils of Presentation College, St George's. Loud cheers from the pressing crowd mingled with a fanfare from the Grenada Police Band and echoes of a cannon salute from nearby Fort George.[3]

The official welcoming party comprised Deputy Governor Keith Alleyne, Q.C. and Mrs. Alleyne, Premier E.M. Gairy and Mrs. Gairy, Mr Joseph Gibbs, Past President of the Senate and father of Dr Bynoe, Mr Winston Masanto, Aide de Camps and Mrs. Clifford Date, private secretary. *The Torchlight* reported that "Grenada's first local-born Governor was given a welcome as warm and sunny as the weather that greeted the occasion". The paper also noted the presence of Dr Bynoe's only sister "Mrs. Josephine Barker and other close relatives from Crochu".[4] As the new Governor stepped ashore in Grenada, there was steel pan music from the Johnny Walker Angel Harps steel orchestra. A new era had begun.

In her first address to the Grenada parliament, Dr Bynoe said:

> Today, June 8th, 1968, history has been made in this beloved island of ours, commonwealth history. We have entered an era of political independence and you have appointed a woman to the high office of Governor of this State. I am deeply conscious of the honour paid to me and to my family, and through me to womanhood throughout the Caribbean and elsewhere. I thank you for the confidence placed

in me and I assure you that I shall (keep) sacred the oaths to which
I have just sworn and as Her Majesty's representative, will, with God's
help, serve faithfully all the peoples of our beloved land."[5]

Dr Bynoe's reference to "an era of political independence" is an
acknowledgment of the fact that although the country was not
independent, it was on its way to achieving that status. Other
Caribbean countries were already independent. For the entire (British) Caribbean, therefore, it was "an era of independence". When I
interviewed Dame Hilda, she noted regretfully that "Eric Gairy had
taken the opportunity to say that he was paying back my father for
services." She regretted this because, as she recalled, various people,
including the veteran journalist Allister Hughes,[6] "made reference to
this subsequently in some (of his) attacks on me."

As the first local-born governor and the first woman governor,
but, also, as a governor appointed under the Gairy administration,
with Gairy's very public statement that he was paying back her father
for services rendered, almost suggesting that she was a stand-in for
her father, Dr Bynoe had to create her own models for the role. She
was in a difficult position, trying to adopt an attitude of political non-
alignment in a situation where those who opposed the Gairy regime
regarded her as giving some legitimacy to his government by her
presence, and those who supported the regime were pleased to
consider her as one of its positive achievements.

From the stories of the times, it is clear that the family to which Dr
Bynoe belonged was very active in Grenadian politics. Five days after
her arrival back in Grenada, it was announced that Greaves James,
husband of Dr Hilda Bynoe's cousin Enid, had been elected President of the Grenada Senate, and that he was succeeding to the office
vacated by Mr Joseph Gibbs, the Governor's father. He had been
nominated for the post by Senator Derek Knight and the nomination
was seconded by Dr Adolf Bierzynski.[7] Considering the family's
involvement in Grenadian politics, Grenadians would see Dr Bynoe
not only as an individual with her own ideas on politics and society
but also as an individual connected to the stories and conflicts of
Grenadian politics. From the beginning, therefore, she was faced
with the challenge of establishing her independence and asserting a
voice that might erase the perception that she would be merely a
client of the regime.

Additionally, as noted in the introduction, 1968, the year of Dr

Bynoe's appointment, was a year of international turmoil. It was a year in which, as Mark Kurlansky writes, "'Negroes' became 'blacks'... The word started out in 1968 as a term for black militants, and by the end of the year it became the preferred term for the people."[8] Even in Grenada, with its intense, inward-looking politics, there was an awareness of such seismic shifts in international black consciousness.

One notes, for example, that in a report just three days after its announcement of Dr Bynoe's arrival on the *Courland Bay* to take up her post, the local newspaper, *The Torchlight*, even as it continued to explore the story of Dr Bynoe and her Grenadian relatives, was also announcing that "James Earl Ray, identified by the FBI as Martin Luther King's killer", had been arrested in London.[9] For younger, increasingly more politically-conscious Grenadians, events at home began to be viewed through the lens of international black assertion

In 1969, the British Queen, Grenada's Head of State given its status as an Associated State, bestowed on Dr Bynoe the honour of Dame Commander of the British Empire. Among its announcements of honours for those in the medical profession, the British Medical Journal had the following:

> D.B.E. (Civil Division) Mrs. Hilda Louisa Bynoe, M.B., B.S. Governor, Grenada. Mrs. Bynoe graduated M.B., B.S. London in 1951 after training at the Royal Free Hospital Medical School. She has held several public service appointments in Guyana, Trinidad, and Grenada, and has practised in London. She became Governor of Grenada in June 1968.[10]

In an article arguing that women leaders in the Third World often owe their rise "more to male dynasties than to militant feminism", H. Chua-Eoan notes that although the rise of women to positions of power was much welcomed by feminists, in truth, leaders such as Corazon Aquino in the Philippines, Benazir Bhutto in Pakistan, Violetta Chamorro in Nicaragua, all had behind them "a powerful man or an influential political dynasty."[11] Chua-Eoan also notes that while one might say these women came to power more because of family connections than because of "proven political skills", as, arguably was the case of Britain's Margaret Thatcher or Israel's Golda Meir, she also argues that:

> "political succession by pedigree... by no means precludes women from brilliantly exercising power. For most of history, it was the only path by which women could come to rule. The pattern is not alien

to the West, where potentates of genius included daughters of kings, such as Elizabeth I of England, their widows, such as Catherine the Great of Russia; and their mothers, such as Eleanor of Aquitaine.[12]

I believe this to be true of Dr Bynoe's position, so that even if Premier Gairy could claim to have offered Dr Bynoe the post because of his association with her father, the evidence is there that she was well equipped to carry out the demands of the job. In the circumstances, how did Dame Hilda function?

Dame Hilda Bynoe's story suggests that she was not just the woman chosen by Premier Gairy to be Governor because he wanted to do a favour to a loyal friend. She was the sum of her experiences as wife, as mother, and as a Caribbean woman at a particular moment in the political and socio-economic development of Grenada and the Caribbean. It is also of importance that she was married to a Trinidadian man, himself visionary, at a particular period of Trinidad's political story. It is not to be taken lightly that Peter Bynoe was able to respond calmly to the attention and accolades given his wife and to say simply to the newspapers that he found himself a man in a unique position and that he would have to wait to see how things would develop. Dr Bynoe's own narrative of her husband suggests that he was unfailingly supportive of her efforts during her governorship.

It was known that Hilda Bynoe had federalist sympathies, that she might be termed pan-Africanist in her perspectives and that she had strong views about gender, and might even be referred to as feminist. Gender politics in Trinidad and Tobago, the middle-class women's social work movement aimed at improving the situation of women and of the working poor, and her friendship with the pioneering Audrey Jeffers: all had an influence on the way she conducted her governorship.

Gloria Payne-Banfield argues that "Dame Hilda had come out of the Trinidad and Tobago of Dr Eric Williams' Best Village Competitions, which assisted in identifying and preserving rich, diverse cultural traditions many of which were linked to a shared Grenadian and Caribbean heritage".[13] There were many experiences on which Dame Hilda, as she soon became popularly known, might be expected to draw. Much of her day-to-day work as Governor is lost from the record, but it is possible to see how she advanced those causes that were dear to her. These included – besides federalism and women's rights – education and culture, and of course the interests of Grenada.

Working Governor
It is clear that Dame Hilda considered herself not simply a ceremonial figure but a working Governor, concerned with the everyday life of the island. She was excited about what she regarded as an opportunity to make practical contributions to Grenada and, indeed, to the Caribbean, of which she saw herself a proud citizen.

Speechwriting
Dame Hilda also had an active role in the preparation of the Crown speech. "I used to write the section of the speech dealing with medicine. Mr Gairy had no objections. He would see it first, of course."[14]

Dame Hilda Bynoe – Federalist
As noted in Chapter One, Dr Bynoe credits Grenada's Theophilus Albert Marryshow with being important to the development of her ideas on West Indian Federation, which as an institution lasted from 1958 to 1962, comprising ten British Caribbean territories – Jamaica, Trinidad & Tobago, Barbados, the four Windward Islands (Grenada, Dominica, St Vincent and St Lucia), and three Leeward Island territories (Antigua, St Kitts-Nevis-Anguilla and Montserrat). After almost a hundred years of colonial discussion about a possible Federation of the West Indies, there were, in the twentieth century, more local voices being raised to promote the idea. Jesse Proctor notes that:

> …support for federation became more widespread and articulate in the Caribbean during and after the first World War. The cry was taken up by emerging nationalist leaders such as T. A. Marryshow of Grenada, who took over Donovan's newspaper in 1915,[15] renamed it *The West Indian,* and throughout the following fifteen years urged regularly through it that the West Indies must be federated."[16]

Many political thinkers of Marryshow's generation worked at popularising the federal idea, connecting it to the most radical elements in the islands.

Under the leadership of these men and others like them, West Indians banded together into Representative Government Associations and Workingmen's Associations in the eastern islands. These organisations staged public meetings and dispatched to London petitions demanding more representative political institutions, a broader franchise, and federation.[17]

These federal ideas, much discussed in Grenada during Hilda Gibbs's childhood,[18] helped to establish in her imagination the idea of a federal future for the British Caribbean islands.

In December 1930, the Secretary of State for the Colonies was asked to summon a conference in Grenada "to formulate a plan for the union of the Leewards and Windwards."[19] The main proponents of this idea considered it a step toward the wider federation of the British Caribbean. While Hilda Gibbs, then nine or ten years, would hardly have been much aware of the details of these discussions, they were part of the climate in which she grew up.

The federal experiment ended in 1962 when Alexander Bustamente's anti-federalist campaign defeated the federalist Norman Manley in a referendum in Jamaica in 1961. As Trinidad's Dr Eric Williams, wearing his historian's hat, summarises succinctly: "The Federation of the West Indies, inaugurated in 1958, collapsed in 1962 with the secession of Jamaica."

As we have seen, Dr Bynoe thought that Dr Williams, in his capacity as leader of the Government of Trinidad & Tobago, had also played a negative role in the collapse of the Federation. Elaborating on his much-publicised conclusion that "one from ten leaves nought," Prime Minister Williams wrote: "Its failure was due to two rival conceptions, Jamaica's weak central government and Trinidad's strong central power."[20] Williams's position was probably also influenced by the victory of the Indian-Hindu led Democratic Labour Party (DLP) in the 1958 Federal elections.

Throughout all the vicissitudes of Caribbean attempts to effect a political union, Dr Hilda Bynoe remained a federalist. She was pleased that, after its establishment in 1958, her father was an elected representative to the Federal Parliament.

Eric Gairy, having been banned from office between 1957-1961 by the British colonial government for driving a steelband through an opponent's political meeting, was not then in parliament,[21] but the friendship between him and Joseph Gibbs continued. During this period, however, Gibbs had shown his independence by not casting his vote within the Federal Parliament in the way that Gairy wanted. Gairy, according to Dr Bynoe, wanted Grenada's representatives, both of whom were from his party, to agree that theirs were floating votes. Joseph Gibbs disagreed. His, he said, was not a floating vote. He would vote with the Federal Party, the party in office at the time. In the event, according to Dr Bynoe, because he did not have a floating vote, Joseph Gibbs ended up being a part of the Federal Party's decision to end the Federation. The Bynoes had supported her father's decision that his vote would be a Federal Party vote. In the event, as she looked back, she said she had always wondered how important was her father's individual vote to the end of the Federation.

The Governor's speeches: West Indian Federation

Many of Dame Hilda's speeches as Governor of Grenada made reference to the importance of Caribbean unity. In an address declaring open a conference of the ECCM (East Caribbean Common Market),[22] an organisation aimed at integrating the economies of the LDC's (Least Developed Countries) of the Eastern Caribbean, Dame Hilda expressed her pleasure that "Grenada has been chosen as the venue for this important meeting, since it has given me the opportunity to be identified with you in this attempt at West Indian unity, an ideal to which my government is very firmly committed." She noted that "the principles and objectives of the Eastern Caribbean Common Market agreement aim at the creation of an economic group which is part of a dream which many of our generation had dreamt – the dream of a West Indian economic and political integration, of a West Indian identity." One notes that for Dame Hilda it was not just a personal dream, but one that "many of (her) generation had dreamt." Making the theme of West Indian unity more explicit, the Governor told the assembled ECCM delegates, "The birth and death of the West Indies Federation was perhaps a historical necessity but many of us continue to believe in the goal of ultimate unity of the West Indian peoples." As Governor of Grenada, which during her tenure as governor had not yet attained full political independence, Dame Hilda was clearly not speaking for Grenada alone, but with a perception of a regional federal destiny. It would certainly have been important to her that this regional (or sub-regional) integration meeting and her responsibility within it came at the very beginning of her tenure as governor.

Throughout her period of office, Dame Hilda seized opportunities to express her views about Caribbean integration. In an address to a 1969 graduating class at the University of Guyana, Dame Hilda warned that:

> The independent Commonwealth Caribbean[23] cannot afford to ignore the islands of the Associated States within the Caribbean area.[24] We are separated by much water and many prejudices, but the outside world views us as one people because the differences between us are so trivial that to the stranger we look alike and no member of a family can take pride in his own advancement while his brothers remain in poverty and obscurity.

Clearly descrying the insularity of new Caribbean nationalisms, Dame Hilda advised students that:

> the intellectual appreciation of the need for regional cooperation, to make a thing of meaning of our independence, will come with the increasing influence of the universities of Guyana and the West Indies.

Her comments urged not an individual island or country advancement but an integrated movement toward Caribbean development, and she wanted the region's university students to appreciate that their role would be important in advancing this cause. She seems to have thought that this was particularly important at a period when various Caribbean countries were not only starting off on journeys as independent nation-states, but also working toward attempts at some form of economic integration. Although a Caribbean Free Trade Area (CARIFTA), was not to be established until 1968, Caribbean leaders like her friend Forbes Burnham in Guyana, along with Errol Barrow in Barbados and Vere Bird in St Kitts-Nevis-Anguilla had agreed on its formation since 1965, before their countries had become independent.[25]

The Governor's speeches: Gender

Another important concern, often raised during her period of office, was gender. Dame Hilda Bynoe seized every opportunity to speak to the male political leaders of the region about woman's participation in Caribbean development and she raised the topic for discussion before the representatives at the 1968 ECCM meeting when she said:

> Much has been said in the last few weeks about my appointment as the first woman Governor of the Commonwealth and all the Caribbean governments and peoples have rejoiced in this appointment. Peoples all over the world have seen it as a recognition by you of woman's readiness to play her part in public affairs.[26]

The implicit question seemed to be: "but was it actually a recognition of women?" Facing the all-male representation of the East Caribbean Common Market, she took the opportunity to tell these representatives, "Gentlemen, Caribbean women are ready and willing to join your deliberations, to (give) you their support in your plans", and to request of them to "make use of (women's) talents, give more of them the opportunity to use the education and skills your governments have made possible for them to acquire."

Connecting the story of women's role in Caribbean development and progress towards a Caribbean federation, she noted that:

> ...very few women were involved in the plans for the old West Indies Federation. Take them into your confidence now and let them be not only passengers but part of the crew which will lead us through all the rough passages ahead to the ultimate goal of West Indies integration.

In 1968, six years after the collapse of the West Indies Federation, and at a time when the Eastern Caribbean was embarking on the establishment of a Common Market, Governor Bynoe was not only promoting the idea of West Indian integration, but suggesting that its failure had something to do with it being a male club of clashing egos. It was an early expression of what the Caribbean historian Hilary Beckles was to conclude later, that: "Nation-states, as hegemonic civic enterprises, functioned essentially as 'boys only clubs'", and "the odd woman was admitted but on terms set out by her brethren".[27]

Beckles further noted the tendency towards tokenism, that "It became fashionable to have one woman in each high office – in the cabinet, judiciary, diplomatic corps, permanent secretariat, and so on." Dame Hilda was not prepared to be a lone token woman, and it is to her credit that she used her voice to protest the exclusion of women from decision making. However, given her position in this period as a lone voice in an all-male club, it is perhaps not surprising that such a denunciation of male cronyism in politics did not make its way to the permanent, popular written historical records, but this performance at the ECCM was not an isolated instance of an attempt to promote women's voices and interests.

Gloria Payne-Banfield records that when a Grenada Women's League was launched in 1969, Dame Hilda "engineered a gathering of outstanding Caribbean women". According to Payne-Banfield, "relying on her numerous contacts, Dame Hilda persuaded Viola Burnham and Desiree Bernard of Guyana, Nesta Patrick (Grenada born) and Yvonne Lucas of Trinidad & Tobago, Anne Liburd of St Kitts & Nevis, among others, to attend."[28] Discussions during this visit resulted in the birth of the Caribbean Association of Women (CARIWA) two years later in Georgetown, Guyana.

Throughout her brief, nearly six years of office, whether her male colleagues and a critical younger generation, unimpressed by her connection with the Gairy regime, recognised it or not, Dame Hilda Bynoe insisted on being more than a fashion.

Visit to St Joseph's Convent

When Governor Bynoe visited the St Joseph's Convent high school in June 1968, in a report titled "Governor Visits her Old School", *The Torchlight,* added the subtitle, "Don't Make Marriage Life's Ambition, pupils advised. Rather Train for Leadership." According to *The Torchlight,* at this event, sixth-form student Miss Merle Collins gave "a formal address of welcome, (outlining) some of the changes which the school had seen since Dr Bynoe left some twenty-nine years (before)".[29]

In her address to the girls, Dr Bynoe regretted the absence of Sister Columba, a nun who had been influential in her own education at the school. She urged training for leadership and advised the young women to prepare for life in "an age of great challenge and great achievement", in which marriage should not be their life's ambition.

This was a significant intervention at a convent school dedicated to the education of young women, committed to giving a broad education, but affected also by the general social context of women's expected role as wives and mothers. Grenada was still a country in which marriage was certainly one of the major goals for young womanhood. She was speaking, too, in a small island community where tertiary education and attendance at university were the exception rather than the norm. Although by then the University of the West Indies (UWI) had been established, with campuses in Jamaica, Trinidad & Tobago and Barbados, for Grenadians and other students from smaller islands, education at the UWI still meant travel from home, with added boarding and other expenses. This meant that university education was by no means a given for those leaving Grenada's high schools with sufficient qualifications. In the year that Hilda Bynoe became governor, an additional scholarship was given, publicised as a special scholarship to be competed for amongst girls only, identifying the year 1968 as having a special significance for the women of Grenada. The scholarship was to be based on performance in the 1968 Island Scholarship examination and would be given under the same conditions and be of the same value as the Island Scholarship. The Island Scholarship was a distinction given to the student who, competing in the Cambridge School Certificate exams (Advanced Level), held at the end of the final year of high school (sixth form, when students were typically aged about 18), had the best grades in the island's secondary schools. At the time, these exams (now replaced by the exams of the Caribbean Examinations Council (CXC)) were graded in England. The Island Scholarship was prestigious and valuable, but gave only one student the opportunity for free university education. That special 1968 scholarship for girls went to a St Joseph's Convent student, my classmate Lois LaGrenade, who went to the University of the West Indies at Mona, Jamaica, to study medicine. As students, we had all competed for this scholarship, quietly aware of its importance, even if we said nothing in conversation.

As I talked to Dame Hilda, I remembered the quiet competition of the period. Even as I'd congratulated my classmate, I'd thought longingly about this scholarship given to one girl in the island. Perhaps every girl who took the exam that year longed to have the scholarship given only to girls. I recall this as I write Dame Hilda's story, tracing her journey from the hills of rural St David's/St Andrew's to the St Joseph's Convent, St George's and eventually to England, to meet future Caribbean leaders and thinkers. When she returned to St Joseph's Convent, she came as one of these leaders, advising students to appreciate the opportunities given them, but to be critical, too, in their consideration of any information received.

Dr Bynoe's address at St Joseph's Convent, the first school visited on her tour of office, suggests that she was prepared to be an influential voice, expressing opinions and proffering advice on situations with which she was well acquainted.

Address to CARIWA

In 1972, in an address to CARIWA (Caribbean Women's Association), the organisation started by the wife of Forbes Burnham in the wake of the Grenada meeting, and patterned after a similar organisation once pioneered by Audrey Jeffers in Trinidad, Dame Hilda advised the organisation to maintain its autonomy and ensure that it kept "out of party political aspirations, party political alignments. The individuals within your organisation should be encouraged into active political life but the organisation itself must be non-partisan, working with the governments of the day but remaining free to offer constructive criticism where necessary." But she also urged members to take regional integration seriously:

> In one respect only do I think CARIWA should clearly state a political creed and this is in the matter of Caribbean regional integration and the social, political and economic independence of the area. No regional association of women in the Caribbean can escape a commitment one way or the other on the matter of integration.

She had been asked by Mrs Burnham not only to give the first address but also to be Patron of the Association.

The Governor posed a question to CARIWA: "Do you accept the status quo, the Caribbean reality of poverty for the many, or are you as an organisation committed to change, committed to development, committed to fair shares for all? Are you committed to Caribbean regional integration?" And not seeing integration mentioned, the Governor pointedly noted, "Your constitution does not answer this last question."

To put CARIWA into historical perspective helps us understand Dame Hilda's frank speaking to the organisation. Caribbean feminist critic Rhoda Reddock contextualised the work of women's organisations generally and CARIWA in particular during this period when she wrote:

> The re-emergence of the women's movement internationally in the late 1960s and early 1970s ushered in a new era in Caribbean women's struggle. Unlike the earlier movement, the impact of this new movement has been broader and touched many more aspects of personal and political life. Interestingly, many of the first women to be influenced were the stalwarts of the traditional women's organisations from the era of the 1950s. It could be said that the new consciousness seeping into the region reminded these older women activists of the marginal position they still held within the political organisations of which they were members and in the governments which their parties formed. Two developments are significant in this regard. In 1970, Viola Burnham, of the People's National Congress of Guyana, called together her colleagues from other parts of the region to form CARIWA – The Caribbean Women's Association – with headquarters in Guyana. This organisation attempted to link the various national-level councils or co-ordinating councils of women to which most of the traditional women's organisations were affiliated.[30]

Dame Hilda's ideas were therefore not formed in isolation. She was part of a group of middle-class Caribbean women concerned with Caribbean politics and development and particularly concerned with women's role in the development of the new and emerging post-colonial states. In that 1972 paper to CARIWA, Dame Hilda emphasised class distinctions between women, the need for women to organise themselves, and also tackled the question of feminist ideology and how Caribbean women might define themselves within the international women's movement. She argued:

> We can give a thought to the women's liberation movement and the militant feminism that accompanies it. The women's liberation movement began as a demand by the women in the metropolitan centres for the right to vote, to own property, the right to equality in the law, and this militant feminist movement spread into Britain's West Indian colonies. But the masses of the peoples of the Caribbean, the men and women, had always been equal in their ignorance, in their poverty, in the degradation of their lives. The women's liberation movement of today is demanding change in the attitude of women, changes in the law, to give to women their just rights, changes which result in mutual respect and admiration between the sexes. The

movement, as I understand it, is fighting for liberation from the traditional attitudes that permit the double standards shown in industry, in politics on the domestic scene. But the Caribbean woman must be careful not to import wholesale the ideas of the metropolitan female liberation movement. Some may not suit us. Their methods of fighting may not be ours, as circumstances dictate. But there are some things towards which all women must work, always bearing in mind that the Caribbean woman's attitude is different from that of her metropolitan sisters. They operate from a position of almost, if not full, employment, and we from a position of mass unemployment. They live in a society of plenty and we are surrounded by poverty.[31]

Here one sees her concern that the challenges facing Caribbean women be understood in historical perspective. She wanted to speak about women's personal lives, about professional women and their participation in the nation's economy. Hilda Bynoe had experienced some of the difficulties about which she spoke. To the 1969 University of Guyana graduating class, she had commented:

Marriage often presents problems for the young career woman who may find herself faced with the necessity of neglecting her own professional life in the furtherance of the interests of her family.

She urged that a marriage between university graduates be thought of in terms of a partnership, with women *and* men sharing responsibility for children and for the furtherance of each other's careers.

Dame Hilda was concerned with making feminist organisation relevant to what she considered Caribbean realities – issues of class, gender discrimination in the workplace and gender inequality as expressed in the domestic space – but recognising that economic exclusion was the experience of the majority of men as well as women in the Caribbean. True to the suspicion of colonial control that had been part of her socialisation, she wanted to be sure that the Caribbean women's movement would not see itself merely as an arm of any movement in Europe or America. She urged CARIWA to set its own agenda, based on its assessments of the experiences of Caribbean women.

Even as we discussed women's organisation in that 1960s period, she put a question to me about women's liberation and her role. She asked: "Did your generation see me as a women's lib?" She wanted to know what our (my generation's) perspectives had been on the question of liberation for Caribbean women, and specifically what terms we used to describe her attitudes toward women's issues. Her use of the term "women's lib" suggests, perhaps, a disparagement of what she considered the "militant" tendencies of some metropolitan feminist organisations, her rejection of a brand of feminism that in its criticism of women's subjugation within the family may be thought to disparage family life. She seemed to want to make it clear that whilst she might critique women's experiences from a feminist perspective, she valued family life. Women working in politics – and this is probably as true in Grenada as elsewhere – have always been conscious that they have to find ways of balancing political life with family responsibilities – as wives, sisters and daughters.

So, suspicious of what she appeared to consider a radical metro-politan feminist model, she urged her Caribbean sisters to understand their reality within what might be described as a liberal feminist framework. As Reddock defines it, "Liberal demands... centred on changes in the socialisation process and education system. They also called for women to be given equal rights and equal opportunities with men to compete evenly in the labour market".[32] Gloria Payne-Banfield states that, in Grenada, Hilda Bynoe "played a pivotal role in catalysing the women to join in groups wherever and whenever necessary to make their contribution in a positive way rather than talking about it." Typical of the kind of interventions made by the middle-class women of early Caribbean women's organisations, Hilda Bynoe encouraged women to become part of whatever organisations were then available for women – the Homemakers' Association and its affiliates, home economics groups, the Young Women's Christian Association (YWCA), the Girl Guides, church organisations.[33]

In the interests of all their peoples, she was convinced that Caribbean nations had to find ways of integrating women into the business of development and make sure that their particular talents were utilised within existing political structures.[34]

During her years as Governor, she also challenged CARIWA to undertake a review of the laws of Caribbean countries in order to determine whether they contained discriminatory legislation against women. She challenged the women of the region to seek means of addressing any gender discrimination present in their countries' constitutions. She was concerned that the postcolonial Caribbean was developing political systems that retained discriminatory atti-tudes toward women in their Constitutions. She protested that:

Both in the Grenada and Barbados Constitution, a person belongs to the country if he or she is born there and a person acquires the right to citizenship through the father, never through the mother. Foreign persons who are living in Barbados acquired British nationality under the British Nationality Act and the wives and children of such men as well as the wives and children of West Indian nationals, these people have rights entrenched in our various constitutions, rights which are denied to the husband and children of the West Indian woman.

In 1972, almost four years into her period of office, and two years before she resigned, Governor Bynoe asked CARIWA to be aware that:

we are all foreigners in respect to each other's territory. A woman married to a fellow West Indian, if she and her family wish to live in her country, will find that her husband and children are without the rights enjoyed by the French or German or Japanese wife and children of her brother. Her family will be subject to work permit requirements, to whatever limitations the law places on aliens with respect to property and so on. Her husband and children would be subject to the possibility of being declared immigrants. Her brother's wife and children have the right of choice to acquire citizenship and all the rights and privileges and obligations pertaining thereto. In effect, daughters of the soil may through marriage suffer discriminatory practices from which their brothers are protected.

Governor Bynoe detailed these facts to CARIWA, concerned to motivate the women's organisation to:

seek to influence attitudes which keep us trapped in our poverty, attitudes which make us accept the double standards which result in female exploitation, attitudes which undermine our confidence in Caribbean things and keep us committed to metropolitan standards and values.

She had, she said, worked to change this in the Grenada Constitution.[35] Because of her intervention, she explained to me, Grenada was the first to make that change to rights through marriage and other Caribbean territories followed.

Others have noted that this was a period when discriminatory legislation against women was being challenged in the Caribbean. Feminist critic Eudine Barriteau has written that during this period and later, more particularly during the 1970s and 1980s, "many Caribbean states removed some of the entrenched legal discriminatory measures against women."[36]

Governor Bynoe was very much a pioneer in that movement. She brought to her office the sensibility of a Caribbean woman who was wife, mother and professional, and also of a Caribbean woman involved enough in the everyday stories of her land to want to claim her inheritance as a Caribbean person.

Culture and Society: Personal Style

As a black woman (and here I use the term that was ascendant during the period), Dame Hilda Bynoe had a special place in the public imagination during that era of Black Power agitation. An iconic figure during the late 1960s, early 1970s, her personal style was always of interest to the public. She was aware that she was an influential figure and she was keen to make use of that influence. In June 1968, the *Trinidad Express* reported her as saying, "I'd like to present the teenage girl with a picture of someone she'd like to be in 30 years' time – a successful, fashionable woman."[37] In 1969, the Governor began wearing the popular Afro hairstyle of the period. Whatever may have been her personal motivations, the style suggested to the public that the first black woman governor had empathy with the Black political thought of this period. In our discussions she gave details that show she had the typical woman's dialogue with herself about her hair and how she would present herself to the public. Her hair had been badly damaged in a hairdressing salon (as quite often happened with the hair-straightening methods of that time) and, no doubt influenced by the discussions of the day about the cultural significance of hair, the Governor took the decision to stop straightening and wear her hair naturally.

As Dr Bynoe considered questions about black women and personal style, she recalled a young woman who used to visit Government House on work assignments. This young woman was, she remembered, always beautifully dressed in African prints and wearing an Afro hairstyle. And then, one day, "she came looking like everybody else." The Governor asked her what had happened, and why she had lost her distinctive look. The young woman explained that she had felt ostracised, that people commented on her "odd" appearance. "They're only jealous," the Governor advised, and proceeded to say that she wanted her hair styled like that young woman's.

In her narrative about personal style, Dame Hilda added that when her sons returned from school (in the United States) for the holidays, they approved. On one occasion (another holiday), when she had briefly reverted to her old hairstyle, they were not enthusiastic. Buoyed, therefore, by family reactions, the Governor took the decision to wear her hair natural. In her position, such a decision could not go unnoticed; she was making a personal statement about style and the African-Caribbean woman.

Theatre, the Arts and Culture

For me, one of the precious memories of the late 1960s, early 1970s was a performance in Grenada of Derek Walcott's play *Dream on Monkey Mountain* (premiered in 1957) and Eric Roach's *Belle Fanto* (premiered in 1966). I remember being more enthralled at the time by the acting and in particular by the figure of Makak than by details regarding the plotlines of these dramas. I didn't know then that Governor Bynoe was responsible for the invitation to Derek Walcott to bring the Trinidad Theatre Workshop and these plays to Grenada. It was certainly something that stirred the imagination of young Grenadians, not then given many opportunities for exposure to quality theatre. It was Gloria Payne-Banfield who told me that, "Dame Hilda used her influence with cultural groups in Trinidad & Tobago to invite them to visit Grenada to perform." In addition to Walcott, the Trinidadian playwright Aubrey Adams brought his play *Ambakaila* (premiered in 1972) and Eugene Joseph brought his dance company.

There was music too. "The Governor's residence (Government House) was the scene of recitals and performances," Payne-Banfield added. "How well I recall a piano recital by famous Trinidadian pianist Winifred Atwell, when the piano from Mt Royal (then the residence of the Premier) was borrowed and a team of men carried the piano carefully through the short cut between the two residences so that its tonal quality would not be spoilt by being transported by truck."

Dame Hilda was also concerned with local culture and the place of traditional African religious practices like the Orisha (then known in Grenada as Shango). She invited some of the known exponents to a discussion in the summer house above the tennis court in the grounds of Government House. For the gathering, she served traditional food – cocoa (locally known as cocoa tea) with bakes and

Dame Hilda Bynoe, Governor of Grenada
Painting by S. Morse Brown (1971),
Photograph courtesy Michael Bynoe

saltfish.[38] Her decision to set up this discussion was an important initiative, though its importance was probably undervalued at the time because a Premier unpopular with the younger generation was also thought to be supportive of traditional African practices. The significance of Dame Hilda's move should be seen in a wider context. Whilst the Caribbean is generally comfortable with its practice of a syncretised Christianity (Christianity influenced by African traditional practices), references to or overt exploration of traditional African spirituality or cosmology is a much more fraught subject. In the 1970s, however, Black was beautiful, and so perhaps traditional Africa was less suspect. In her willingness to explore the local and to move to a closer understanding of aspects of African culture as it existed in Grenada, Governor Bynoe was certainly innovative and forward-thinking. She was always willing to struggle for what she considered collective self-esteem in the face of colonial conditioning. Later, in her creative work, she wrote:

> We learned to read and to write. We wrote essays, sang songs and dreamed dreams of White Christmas, putting snow on imported, foreign Christmas trees. We sang songs of praise about a land of hope and glory, not our own land, and even today, Tarzan is the children's hero and not the Black Prince, not the Prince of the Watutsis.
>
> Figures of mirth and ridicule were black men in those days – the Rochesters and the Stepin Fetchits having to play roles stereotyping the black man as fool and rogue and bottom-licker. In films and on stage they were made to be the butt of stupid jokes that white men gave and black men had to laugh at. The Black Man standing full ten feet but had to make himself laugh at their asinine jokes.[39]

These narratives show how interested Governor Bynoe was in the cultural life of the country, in promoting Caribbean theatre and in pulling from out of the shadows the African inheritance in the Caribbean.

Marketing Grenada

Governor Bynoe clearly saw that an important part of her role was promoting Grenada. For instance, she concerned herself with developing a market for Grenada's flora, and was instrumental in working toward an agreement with Martinique for selling anthuriums. Although the idea seems not to have been popular with Premier Gairy, Dame Hilda believed that this horticultural project had taken root in Grenada. In this venture, she had the support of Ms May Regis, a cousin who worked in Grenada's Ministry of Social Services. With the help of Ms Regis, the Governor organised a group of local suppliers and Ms Regis would collect and take the anthuriums to Government House, where they were prepared for sale. There was an outlet in St George's for this product and also a market in Trinidad, where there was a demand for hybrid anthuriums. The fact that the anthuriums would be prepared for sale at Government House is another indication of the hands-on approach of a Governor knowledgeable about and interested in the details of everyday existence.

Home for the Handicapped

In 1970, Dame Hilda Bynoe spoke at the Kennedy Home, then located at Richmond Hill, St George's. She noted that, in 1968, Professor Michael Beaubrun, Professor of Psychiatry at the University of the West Indies, wrote to the Carmelite sisters about constructing in Grenada a home for handicapped children and about the need for adequate skills to run this home. The result was that in September 1969 Sister Mary Joseph went from Guyana to Grenada to help establish the Kennedy Home.

Expo '69 and Grenada Politics

In a 5th April, 1969 address at the opening of Grenada's CARIFTA (Caribbean Free Trade Area) Expo '69,[40] a trade and cultural extravaganza planned by Premier Eric Gairy, with important architectural contributions from the Governor's husband, Peter Bynoe, Governor Bynoe coined the phrase "expo tempo" and extolled the existence of this tempo which began "among the workers in True Blue[41] and spread to the road builders along the route from Pearls airport[42] to the construction workers preparing the routes for the hundreds and the thousands we hope to attract."

She noted that, "there have been some who did not believe in our project," and suggested that "they have been proven wrong and the benefits to our country from this exposition (are) not to be measured by the flow of visitors of the last few months. To me, the greatest gain that CARIFTA Expo '69 has brought to Grenada is the highlighting of our people's capacity for hard work and devoted service in their country's interest and secondly, the proof it has given of the financial benefits from improved output." She expressed the opinion that this exposition planned by the government of Eric Gairy was "a project well executed" and that "Expo '69 has given to us this Easter more spending money than ever before."

It was a project in which both Governor Bynoe and her husband took a great deal of interest. Peter Bynoe's architectural skills were invaluable to the government for the construction of cottages and other buildings needed for the grand exposition. Peter Bynoe had the opportunity, with Expo '69, to make use of his professional skills and become occupied with his own project. He had participated in a Canadian Expo and so had the experience to give high quality assistance in Grenada. Indeed, Expo '69 provided an opportunity for Peter Bynoe and Dame Hilda to work together professionally in areas in which each was interested. CARIFTA, the reason for the exposition, was the symbol of regional integration, a subject about which Dame Hilda was passionate. The construction of the village would be Peter Bynoe's concern. However, and this was critical in the events that led to her resignation, the Governor's supportive speeches about Expo '69 served to identify her more closely with the Gairy government. Eager to see the project succeed, she chided the nay-sayers and affirmed the wisdom of her government. She used her influence to "borrow" the renowned Trinidadian theatrical lighting designer George Williams to assist with the production of the staged shows at the "Nutmeg Theatre", constructed for the Expo '69 extravaganza.[43] In our discussions, she seemed particularly excited in talking about Expo '69. At the time, in her excitement, she must have appeared to identity completely with the government of Eric Gairy. It was "our project", and it had given "us" more spending money in Grenada than ever before.

As Governor, Dame Hilda clearly considered that she had a responsibility to promote Grenada abroad. She was conscious, too, of the fractious nature of world relations in 1968 and the challenges posed to a small country. She regarded her role as representing a much-loved Grenada, not so much in its individual island or country identities, as in its Caribbean totality. She belonged to Grenada, Trinidad and the Caribbean, and represented a quintessentially Caribbean vision.

Endnotes

1. Excerpt from "We never knew St George's", Hilda Bynoe, *I woke at Dawn* (Port of Spain: Hanz' On Publishers, 1996).
2. *The Trinidad Guardian,* Friday June 7, 1968.
3. *The Trinidad Guardian,* op. cit.
4. *The Torchlight,* Friday June 7, 1968.
5. From Dame Hilda Bynoe's personal files.
6. Grenadian journalist Allister Hughes reported extensively on the anti-Gairy demonstrations of the late 1960s and early 1970s. After the January 21st demonstrations in which Rupert Bishop, Maurice Bishop's father, was killed at the union headquarters by Gairy's security forces, Hughes fled Grenada and was given refuge with friends in other islands. "Attacks" against the Governor may have been part of the critique of the Gairy regime of the period.
7. *The Torchlight,* Monday June 10, 1968.
8. Mark Kulansky, *1968: the year that rocked the world.*
9. *The Torchlight,* Wednesday June 12, 1968.
10. "Medical New Year Honours", *British Medical Journal*, 11 January, 1969. p. 111.
11. H. Chua-Eoan, "All in the Family", *Time,* Fall 1990. Volume 136, Issue 19.
12. H. Chua-Eoan, op. cit..
13. Interview with Gloria Payne-Banfield, November 2011.
14. Traditionally, the "Crown Speech" is an address to Parliament delivered once a year by the representative of the Crown. The speech typically outlines the government's plans for the coming year.
15. William Galway Donovan was a Grenadian, one of the earliest Caribbean persons to call for a federation of the West Indies. He was editor of the *Federalist and Grenada People,* a precursor to *The West Indian,* from about 1905 to 1915.
16. Jesse H. Proctor Jr., "The Development of the idea of Federation of the British Caribbean Territories", *Revista de Historia de America*, No. 39 (June 1955), pp. 61-105.
17. Jesse Proctor, op. cit, p. 77.
18. One writer comments, "Between 1921 and 1946, many ideas were put forward concerning the closer association of the British

West Indies, although federation of the British West Indies did not become a practical possibility until after World War II. (See Masahiro Igarachi, *Associated Statehood in International Law,* p. 117). See also www.caricom.org.

19. Proctor, op.cit., p. 88.

20. Eric Williams, *From Columbus to Castro: The History of the Caribbean 1492-1969* (London: Andre Deutsch, 1970), p. 475.

21. See Merle Collins, "Grenada: A Political History, 1950-1979", Ph.D. thesis, University of London, 1990 p. 270. See also *The West Indian,* Saturday 20 July 1957, Vol. 42, No. 133, p. 2. Both sources detail the following: "A 1957 amendment to the Legislative Council (Elections) Ordinance, 1951, extending the provisions dealing with illegal practices during the period of the election campaign, included the stipulation that 'Any person who is convicted of any offence declared to be an illegal practice under this or any other action of this Ordinance shall, in addition to any other penalty for such offence, be incapable during a period of five years from the date of his conviction – (a) of being registered as an elector voting at any election; and (b) of being elected a member of the Legislative Council, or if elected before his conviction, of retaining his seat as such member."

22. After the collapse of the Federation of the West Indies, there were several efforts at regional or sub-regional integration. The ECCM was an attempt by those referred to as the LDCs, the Less Developed Countries of the Caribbean, the smaller islands, to form a Customs Union. Meantime, on 1st May 1968, CARIFTA (a Caribbean Free Trade Area) had come into being with original signatories Antigua, Barbados and Guyana later joined by Trinidad. The ECCM was the result of LDC dissatisfaction with the provisions of CARIFTA. The LDCs finally joined CARIFTA on 1 July, 1968. For a discussion of Caribbean integration, see W. Andrew Axline, "Integration and Development in the Commonwealth Caribbean", *International Organization*. Vol. 32, No. 4. pp. 953-973.

23. Trinidad and Jamaica became independent countries in 1962. Guyana gained its status as an Independent country in 1966. Grenada and other islands of the Eastern Caribbean were not yet independent.

24. Following the collapse of the Federation of the West Indies in 1962, Trinidad and Jamaica became independent territories. The smaller islands of the Caribbean became, constitutionally, Associated States having responsibility for their own internal affairs, with Britain retaining responsibility for external affairs and defence.

25. See Brereton & Higman, ed., *General History of the Caribbean,* Vol.5, (Unesco, 2004), p. 361.

26. Dame Hilda's personal files: Governor's Address to the ECCM, 1968.

27. Hilary Mc. D. Beckles, "Historicizing Slavery in West Indian Feminisms", *Feminist Review.* No. 59: *Rethinking Caribbean Difference* (Summer 1998), p. 49.

28. Interview with Gloria Payne-Banfield, November 2011.

29. *The Torchlight*, Friday June 21, 1968.

30. Rhoda Reddock, "Women's Organizations and Movements in the Commonwealth Caribbean: The Response to Global Economic Crisis in the 1980s", *Feminist Review.* No. 59. *Rethinking Caribbean Difference* (Summer, 1998), pp. 57-73.

31. 1972 Address to CARIWA, copy obtained from Dame Hilda Bynoe's private library.

32. Rhoda Reddock, "Feminism and Feminist Thought: An Historical Overview" in Patricia Mohamed & Catherine Shepherd, ed., *Gender in Caribbean Development* (Kingston: The University of the West Indies Press, 1999), p. 70.

33. Interview with Gloria Payne-Banfield, November 2011.

34. For further discussions of the liberal feminist approach, see Reddock, op.cit. and Patricia Mohamed, *Rethinking Caribbean Difference, Feminist Review:* Number 59 (Summer 1998).

35. Grenada became an Independent nation on 7 February, 1974, one year after the precipitate departure of Governor Bynoe. She would be speaking here of the preparations made for independence.

36. Eudine Barriteau, "Theorizing Gender Systems and the Project of Modernity in the Twentieth-Century Caribbean, *Feminist Review* No. 59: *Rethinking Caribbean Difference* (Summer 1998), pp. 186-210.

37. *The Trinidad Express,* Sunday June 2, 1968.

38. Interview with Gloria Payne-Banfield, November 2011.

39. Excerpt from "We never knew St George's", Hilda Bynoe, *I Woke at Dawn.*
40. For information about the beginning of Grenada's participation in the attempt at regional integration known as CARIFTA, see note 19 above .
41. Site in South St George's which was the venue for Carifta Expo '69.
42. The Grenada airport, now an international airport located in south St George's, was at this time a small airport located in the village of Pearls, St Andrew's, in the northeast of the island.
43. Interview with Gloria Payne-Banfield, November 2011.

CHAPTER SEVEN
DISRESPECT – THE END

As Governor Dame Hilda Bynoe tried to make her mark on the times and to effect the kinds of changes she would like to see within the country, she could not escape the fact that the country's elected Premier Eric Gairy was unpopular with an increasingly vociferous cross-section of the Grenada population. Unfortunately for the Governor, this unpopularity had an impact on attitudes towards her. The last days of her tenure as Governor of Grenada cannot be effectively discussed without putting the story into the context of the times – of what was happening politically in Grenada and its environs.

In the 1970s, young people demonstrating against the Gairy regime and its perceived authoritarianism and corruption were determined that independence would not find Grenada with Gairy in office as prime minister. Following the requisite meetings in London, the date of Grenada's independence was set at February 7, 1974. Still at work, Governor Bynoe was again instrumental in "borrowing" the services of another Trinidadian, John Cupid, to assist with the staging of a grand historical pageant planned for the Independence celebrations.[1] Meanwhile, in early 1974, anti-government demonstrators marched through the streets, anxious to show the world – in particular, Britain – that Grenada was ungovernable with Eric Gairy in office.

Internationally, the 1970s were a period of economic depression: the oil crisis had particularly serious effects on small, developing economies.[2] The Caribbean Community (CARICOM), an organisation established in 1973 with the membership of the four independent countries of the region – Barbados, Guyana, Jamaica and Trinidad & Tobago[3] – felt that in the context of the international situation, there was no reason for optimism. Caricom Secretary-General William Demas referred to 1974 as "the year of adversity".[4] In neighbouring Trinidad, Prime Minister Eric Williams, still engaged in managing the political discontents that remained after the 1970 Black Power uprising, even with Trinidad's relatively good prospects in the region because of its oil revenues, commented that "in the world that is taking shape in 1974, it is quite clear that this is one New Year's day when it is fatuous to wish anyone a happy and prosperous New Year."[5]

In Grenada, the Gairy government, already pressured by fallout from the international economic crisis, was further beleaguered by strikes and demonstrations held to protest the Government's method of handling dissent. With the new governmental authority afforded by the 1967 Constitution, there had been increasing allegations of repression. During this period, several groups were formed to challenge the Gairy regime. One group, the New Jewel Movement, emphasising the need for radical change, caught the imagination of Grenada's youth. JEWEL (Joint Endeavour for Welfare, Education and Liberation), one of the groups that later merged to form the New Jewel Movement, engaged in the kind of civil disobedience that Gairy had used to his advantage in the workers' struggles of 1951. Formed in St David's by a Howard University trained economist Unison Whiteman, JEWEL led a protest against an absentee English owner, Lord Brownlow, who cordoned off land on the LaSagesse estate in St David's, preventing the residents' access to a local beach. This and similar types of action were popular with the people. Quickly, the New Jewel Movement, comprising a merger between JEWEL and another group, MAP (Movement for Assemblies of the People), itself the result of an earlier merger between Maurice Bishop's MACE (Movement for the Advancement of Community Effort) and Kendrick Radix's Committee of Concerned Citizens. Bishop and Radix, lawyers returned from study in England, began organizing, particularly among a disenchanted youthful population. Gairy was now seen as the representative of an old order of union bosses who had emerged with the coming of adult suffrage. As Independence approached, this old guard was being challenged. The 1973 New Jewel Manifesto declared:

> We reject as a total pappy show[6] the present 1967 and the proposed 1974 Constitutions which were imposed on us by the British government. It is a shameful reflection that it took three trips to London to discuss the 1974 Constitution and all that resulted is three minor changes from the Associated States Constitution of 1967. In effect Englishmen drafted the laws which are to govern us. We had no say.[7]

At an outdoor NJM rally held at Seamoon, St Andrew's, and allegedly attended by 10,000 people,[8] Premier Gairy was "tried" by the people and called upon to resign or face a total shutdown of the country beginning 18 November 1973. The regional press began to take notice of the NJM and to report the NJM's assertion that, given the corruption of the Gairy regime, the people (led by the NJM) would have to seize power since the Gairy government would not allow itself to be voted out of office. Gairy responded by accusing the group of threatening "treason"[9] against a "democratically and constitutionally elected government".[10] On 18 November, 1973, NJM leaders visiting Grenville to discuss a planned strike were ambushed and badly beaten, allegedly by police both regular and "secret". Six NJM members were arrested. Following the Grenville beatings and arrests, students from five secondary schools stayed away from classes. Grenadian students at the Cave Hill (Barbados) campus of the University of the West Indies demanded release of the prisoners and pledged solidarity with the people of Grenada "in the struggle against tyranny".[11] Subsequently, anti-Gairy strikes and demonstrations were more broad-based. There emerged a "National Unity Council" comprising various disaffected groups, which began to take control of the protest. In demonstrations, crowds chanted, "Gairy must go!"

November 18, 1973, the day on which members of the New Jewel Movement were beaten at Grenville, was the birthday of Dame Hilda Bynoe. The day before, the Government House driver, Sergeant Stroude, had driven Dame Hilda to her family home in Crochu so she could spend the evening with her father. There, she said, "People began ringing me, telling me about the events that had taken place in Grenville." She was not an inaccessible expatriate Governor. She was a part of the community, open to and pulled into all its emotional entanglements. People expected to have, and got, more access than they would have to an expatriate representative. Now Dame Hilda asked, "Who answers the phone (when they call on that day)? Hilda plus everybody. Who calls the Governor? Everybody was calling. Everyone wanted to know what I would do." Explaining her journey towards a response to this crisis situation, she explained, "I was strongest when Peter wasn't there. Once he was there, I leant on him."

She recalled "the burden of everything I felt that night". She recalled that those beaten had left the island to go to Trinidad for treatment. She recalled that as a result of that night, NGOs (Non-Government Organisations) and private sector organisations began to agitate. Everyone wanted to see the Governor. She responded that there was nothing she could do. Eventually, they went to see Premier Eric Gairy directly.

The Committee of 22, a multi-sector organisation formed during this period, agitated for the establishment of a Commission of Enquiry, which, they insisted, must be appointed by the Governor. Premier Gairy was feeling sufficiently pressured to agree. Trying to find someone from as far away as possible (within the Caribbean) to lead the Commission, Dame Hilda, with the advice of her husband, decided on Jamaica's Sir Hubert Duffus, retired Chief Justice. Her quiet insertion of "with Peter's advice" is a reminder that this Governor, operating in a small state with few resources, had no official team of advisors. In this time of stress, she listened to what her husband had to say. Peter Bynoe, generally an unobtrusive presence, helped her to think about the variables.

They also chose Mr Aubrey Fraser, an eminent Jamaican jurist who had served in an important 1970 case in Trinidad & Tobago, and a representative from the church. The opposition at first seemed satisfied with the work of the Commission, although, according to Dr Bynoe, the appointees were later criticised as being of "one family". Once the Commission had been appointed, the volatile situation in Grenada visibly eased. Then Eric Gairy made what the Governor assessed as a "big blunder", by appearing before the Commission without legal representation. Christmas 1973 came, and the Commissioners went home, hoping to reconvene after the holiday. Dr Bynoe explained that they had no response from Eric Gairy when they asked for a date for reconvening. The Duffus Commissioners left and did not return to Grenada, and the marches resumed. Aubrey Fraser did return, but his purpose was to enquire of Dame Hilda what the situation was and if she felt threatened.

Meantime, neighbouring Caribbean governments were occupied with their own problems. Facing dissent, Trinidad's Prime Minister Eric Williams had threatened to resign. In neighbouring St Vincent, the James Mitchell government, with a one-seat majority, was fighting off a no-confidence motion proposed by opposition Labour Party leader, Milton Cato. In the United States, the Nixon government was embroiled in Watergate. Events in Grenada, while they had their own character because of Grenada's history and the personalities involved, joined events taking place in a world in transition. In the particular local situation, there seemed no way for the Governor to be able to remain aloof from and untouched by the anti-colonial, anti-imperialist thrust of the new, youthful opposition NJM and the anti-establishment instincts of students and young people disenchanted with the actions, decisions and attitudes of figures of authority. Dame Hilda Bynoe was inevitably caught up in the battle of emotions between Premier Gairy and the Grenadian public.

For Dame Hilda, those last moments in office are an unpleasant memory. She explained it like this: "Demonstrators had been marching along the road past Government House and chanting 'Belmar[12] must go and Gairy too!' And I would stand on the balcony and look at them." She was conscious that her son, Roland, wanted to join the protest marches and that he only held back in deference to her. And suddenly, one morning, she reported: "like a command band passing, they caught sight of me. 'Belmar must go, Gairy must go and the Governor too', they chanted. This was the beginning of the end for me. Peter was chairing a meeting on the Independence celebrations. My son Roland, on holiday from boarding school, was sitting on the roots of an old mahogany tree." Dr Bynoe remembered it in detail, the way the light of a rainbow filtered through the leaves of the mahogany tree, and she remembered, too, that she felt disrespected and considered that she was the cause of disrespect to the Bynoe name. For her, it was over. There was her son, wanting to be in the demonstration, seated on the root of the mahogany tree. There was she, Hilda Gibbs, now Bynoe, disrespected and denied. "I knew I was going. Nobody could make me stay, not even Peter. He never tried to influence me one way or the other in that regard. For me, it was if something … a weight … was off my shoulders." She reflected, in our conversations, that she had originally told Premier Gairy that she would be in Grenada for five years. When he announced that he was going for Independence, it was a two-fold thing. "To be honest," she says, "I liked the idea of being the first Governor-General".[13] She added, "I had told him that I would stay on in the first period following Independence, but that I would then leave. Now, I contacted him to say that I would not be staying. I went public right away, in case there was any effort to make me change my mind. I called the international press and told them that I had given the Premier a letter." She explained further that she had written that "unless he, Mr Gairy, and the opposition, assured me that they wanted me to remain as Governor of Grenada, I was leaving. I gave a copy of that letter to the international press. By that night, Gairy announced that he had sacked me. I had by then also contacted the British Government representative in Grenada."

Grenadian organisations made varying responses and Dame Hilda kept these responses in her files. The press released the Governor's decision, and several people heard her address on local Radio Grenada. A letter from George Solomon, General Secretary of the Grenada Veterans' Association, said that he had been directed to advise that "the members are unanimous that you should remain in office."[14] A similar letter, dated 12th January 1974, came from the St George's Conference of the St Vincent de Paul Society: "I hereby wish to inform you that the members deeply appreciate your service to Grenada, and ardently request that Your Excellency remain in office." From the offices of the New Jewel Movement, then in determined opposition to Gairy, came a letter signed by E.A. Carberry, Publications Secretary of the NJM, dated January 12, 1974, and responding, according to the writer, to "your letter dated the 11th instant". It advised that "It is our firm conviction that you no longer enjoy the confidence of the people of Grenada. As such, we welcome your declared intention not to remain in office 'beyond the wishes of the people of Grenada' and now look forward to your immediate resignation." The letter further advised the Governor that she would be welcome to remain in Grenada as a medical practitioner, "serving your people in a practical and meaningful way." The beating of NJM members at Grenville, St Andrew's had precipitated the crisis and the NJM was not about to let the Governor down lightly. The tone of the letter suggests a perception that the Governor occupied a privileged position while the majority of people were in situations of need.

Dame Hilda contacted the deputy British High Commissioner, who was on the island, and asked him to Government House for a meeting. In keeping with the protocol expected of her office, Dame Hilda gave the deputy High Commissioner a letter, to be sent off to the British Queen, requesting Her Majesty's "permission to retire".

She recalled that, by this stage, "negative activities began to unfold". On the radio, she and her husband heard the Premier calling on his security forces to go to his home at Mt Royal, on the hillside above where she resided at Government House. Soon, after the security forces arrived, the sound of cheering and applause could be heard from the Mt Royal meeting.

Dame Hilda recalled details from those last hours as Governor of Grenada. Greaves James, President of the Senate, dropped by. Greaves James was not only President of the Senate but also a relative by marriage, husband of her cousin Enid, who, after the death of her mother, Duxie, had been brought up as a sister to Hilda and Josephine Gibbs. As President of the Senate, Greaves James was one of those in a position to act as Governor should the appointed Governor be absent from the country. He was, however, second in line to Mr Leo De Gale, and the Governor took the opportunity to prepare letters appointing Leo DeGale as Acting Governor and asked Greaves James to convey the letter advising of this to the Premier's residence at Mt Royal.

On 21st January, 1974, Dame Hilda Bynoe left the country. As they drove away from Government House, the Bynoes were intercepted by a messenger who said that the situation was becoming more dangerous, and that someone had been killed. Peter Bynoe said, "This no longer has anything to do with us", and the Bynoes drove on, out of St George's, towards the airport, which was then located in the village of Pearls, in the north of the island. One notes, as Dr Bynoe tells her story, that here again, she says, unusually, "Peter said". The impression is that generally Peter Bynoe did not intervene, but that he spoke in those difficult days, when a crisis had to be managed. It later came to light that the person killed on that day was the father of Maurice Bishop, one of the leaders of the New Jewel Movement, who was later to become Prime Minister of Grenada during the short-lived period of revolution. Mr Rupert Bishop had apparently been killed by the forces of the Premier as they stormed the union building where he stood in the doorway, protectively shielding demonstrating school children who had fled from police violence to take refuge inside the building.

The *Trinidad Guardian* reported that the Governor's departure came after "a massive march through the island's capital, in support of the demand for the resignation of the Government of Premier Eric Gairy."[15]

Seventeen days after her departure, Grenada, "still shrouded in shock and gloom, and with no electricity",[16] was accorded the status of Independent nation in the British Commonwealth of Nations and, on February 7, 1974, Premier Gairy became Prime Minister Gairy. Associated Statehood had provided for the grant of independence should the state request it and the state had requested it.[17] Caldwell Taylor puts Grenada's journey toward independence in historical perspective:

> The Associated State of Grenada, Carriacou and Petite Martinique became formally decolonised on 7 February 1974. Formal decolonisation – "Independence" – was not the outcome of an independence struggle waged by the Grenadian people; it was instead an act of self-serving "generosity" on the part of the retreating colonial power. The British, as Eric Williams (1911-1981) once pointed out, had sucked the orange dry and subsequently became mortally afraid of landing on the peel. This debilitating fear of "stepping on the peel" was a key reason Britain pressed its West Indian "possessions" into the 1958 Federation. From the standpoint of the British and also from that of the major West Indian political leaders of the day, federation was "the only enabling formula which would allow (the islands) to meet the test for full self-government and independence". But the Federation came undone in just three years and the grand idea of West Indian decolonisation en masse perished with it. In the days following the collapse of the Federation, the British warmed up to the idea of granting independence to individual West Indian territories."[18]

The end of Hilda Bynoe's governorship was both a personal trauma and part of a broader political trauma in the small Caribbean nation. Demonstrators, in their anxiety to be rid of Premier Eric Gairy, were ready to sacrifice anyone who might be identified with his government. Although Governor Bynoe was not being personally targeted, her government was and so she, too, was being rejected, not just by implication, but directly, when demonstrators named her. Her response to this was that she felt "disrespected" when demonstrators chanted "and Bynoe too", meaning that "Bynoe must go too". It was a response, she argued, to the disrespect meted out to the Bynoe name. Perhaps it was more than this. Dame Hilda's story shows that she was heavily invested in the country and the region and her sense of rootedness and belonging to the country had also taken a blow. She could not respond as an expatriate (white British) Governor might, because she had a personal emotional investment in the country. Her ancestors had witnessed her investiture. She would not remain when she had been asked to leave.

Early in this biography, I mentioned Thomas Perronet Thompson,

British Governor of Sierra Leone from 1808-1810, because I found it interesting to compare elements of the two stories. With an education at a British grammar school and at Queen's College, Cambridge, Thompson was the son of a Hull merchant. At the time that he was given the Governorship of Sierra Leone, he was a friend of William Wilberforce. Later, he lost his post partly because he was an outspoken critic of British Government policy and had criticised his friend Wilberforce for supporting a policy of supposedly freeing Africans liberated from slave ships and then having them serve a period of apprenticeship as "freed Africans" in Sierra Leone. Thompson continued to contribute to his nation in various ways, serving in the British army in India. There, too, he was conscious of the roles of British officials as outsiders to the lands they served in. As early as the first part of the nineteenth century, as an agent of colonial control, Thompson understood that:

> ...the position of an European in India, really excludes him from an accurate knowledge of the social and domestic condition, the opinions and habits, of the people. Among them he never dwells; he never meets them as equals or companions; their habitual thoughts and passions are not divulged to him; in his presence they neither do nor say what they would do or say in his absence; before him they have a part to act, a point to carry, an end to gain. It is only by a remote influence that the legislator reaches the circle of home.[19]

When forced out of office, he went home to England, but Hilda Bynoe's home was the Caribbean. As the first local-born Governor, her 20th century experience was a very different one. She was invested in the Caribbean stories in a way that white expatriate colonial governors could not be and she had to teach herself how to operate in this singular position. Writing in the nineteenth century, Thompson had noted that "At present no Englishman can have a permanent interest in the prosperity of India; he is a foreigner not planted there, nor held by any of the ties of attachment to soil or country".[20] This gives particular resonance to Hilda Bynoe's story about being on a plum tree in the land where her ancestors were buried when her imminent appointment as Governor was announced on local radio. With her husband's support, she struggled to find a woman's way of existing in a political environment that she imagined would be familiar because of her liberal democratic drive to promote gender equality of achievement and reform of the existing system of gender relations.

Some Grenadian memories of Dame Hilda's actions during this period record the warmth and easy flow of her personality. Some of those who demonstrated remember the songs that they sang:

> Bye Bye Hilda, Bye Bye Hilda
> We hate to see you go.

Some remember her at first waving to demonstrators from the balcony of Government House. Some who worked in government offices during the period of her tenure remember her as "a fun person", easy-going, "not stiff and hoity toity".[21]

Dame Hilda's position as Governor was compromised by the fact that she had been suggested for her post by an unpopular regime at a period when anti-colonial, anti-imperialist ideas were being much discussed by the youth. It was impossible for her to remain untouched. In her speeches, she, as a matter of protocol, referred to "my government", so she was, inevitably, identified with the regime. The ordinary person was not looking for details, simply identifying figures in positions of authority who might be expected to use their authority to help change the situation. It is doubtful whether Governor Bynoe would have been able to influence Eric Gairy's political decisions at this period, but the demonstrators were not concerned with such details. Given the tenor of the time, the critiques of British rule and the 1967 Constitution, even the usefulness of the post of Governor was the subject of local political debate and this attitude was reflected in chants and in the wording of some demonstrators' placards. The popular commentary was that the Governor would like to hear from the public whether they wanted her to stay or go. It is interesting to consider both Dame Hilda Bynoe's story and the reports from observers and participants during that period. Grenadian historian George Brizan concludes that the Governor may have been overwhelmed by the massiveness of the demonstrations.[22]

Whatever may have been Premier Gairy's assessment of Dame Hilda's departure, there were ministers of government, the Hon. George Hosten and Hon. Derek Knight, who sought to ensure that, in those troubled times, she travelled safely. When the Bynoes got to the airport,[23] they discovered that airport workers were on strike. At the airport were Messrs. Derek Knight and George Hosten, come to see them off. Derek Knight, it must be remembered, was a personal friend of the Bynoes predating the Gairy era, and George Hosten, Minister of Finance, had become a friend. Dr Bynoe remembers that Messrs. Knight and Hosten commandeered a plane that happened to arrive at the airport and "ordered the pilot to take us to St Vincent." There were other people at Pearls airport that day, some waiting to say goodbye to the departing Governor during this tense period of anti-Gairy demonstrations. "The Deputy British High Commissioner and his wife were up there to see me off." Having already forwarded to the Queen her request for release from her duties as Governor, Dr Bynoe was leaving before receiving a response. In the event, she left in place an Acting Governor, Leo De Gale. The plane commandeered by Hosten and Knight took the Bynoes to St Vincent, and, from there, a plane was chartered by Hosten to get them to Trinidad.

Of her arrival in Trinidad Dr Bynoe reported: "(When) I arrived in Trinidad from Grenada, I was heading for Guyana." She had been invited to Guyana by the then Prime Minister, Forbes Burnham, whom they had known in London. Friends and well-wishers from all over the world were offering the couple refuge in this difficult time, but Dame Hilda wanted to be in the Caribbean. In Guyana, the Bynoes stayed at first with the Guyanese Prime Minister and then moved on to be with other friends in Guyana, Hazel and Frank Williams. Confirmation of the Queen's permission to vacate the office of Governor came while the Bynoes were in Guyana. The actual acceptance of Dame Hilda's resignation was conveyed via a telephone message from the British High Commission in Guyana. Shortly after this, the family returned to Trinidad.

The memory of one incident during that worrisome, depressing period remained with Dame Hilda. A maid at the residence of the Guyanese Prime Minister started a conversation, showing that she cared about this woman who seemed out of sorts. Dame Hilda recalled it as an encounter full of warmth and understanding from an unknown woman, not of her religion, who allowed the ex-Governor to relax, weep in her arms, and who prayed for her spirit's recovery while she wept. Dame Hilda explained, "God was coming to me through her, and I was able to dry my tears and feel better and get on with life… I had to mention this," she said, "because I have never been able to forget… At this moment, if she is alive, she must be very, very old, and if she is not alive, then may her soul rest in peace."

Dame Hilda remembered the immediate post-Grenada period as

a period of "extreme distress", of depression so acute that it must have been "clinical". It was the occasion for a review of her life's choices, of professional achievements and disappointments. A woman well able to contribute to the development of her country had had her purpose undermined by the circumstances and attitudes of the time. At a disadvantage because of the circumstances of her appointment and departure, Dame Hilda had even failed to secure the traditional pension given to ex-Governors for their years of service. She was the first local Governor and, shortly after she left office, it became the business of the now independent Grenadian government, and no longer that of the British Crown, to allocate pensions to its ex-Governors.[24] Prime Minister Gairy was unhappy about the circumstances of her departure and therefore, apparently, not inclined to ensure that Dame Hilda was allocated a pension. The matter has never been rectified.

With her story circumscribed in the popular imagination by her years of service during the Gairy regime, students and researchers of Grenadian history seem unsure about how to categorise her. In *Women in Grenadian History,* Nicole Phillip concludes: "The office of Governor is a political appointment. This must be taken into consideration when analysing the role of Dame Hilda Bynoe in Grenada's history."[25] When that perspective is taken, it seems that the odds were not in her favour. On the one hand, as Governor she did her best to promote Grenada, but this inevitably aligned her with the government, and though she seems to have concluded that it was wise to keep out of the political entanglements occasioned by the performance of the Gairy regime, this was not a distinction that many Grenadians were prepared to make. In the event, the care with which historians treat her period of office may be symptomatic of a tension between liking for the Governor personally and distaste for the Government that had brought her to office. Nicole Phillip's 2010 publication concludes: "It could be argued that her post was useless since she did little to assist the people when complaints were brought to her attention, and that her speeches held an apologetic tone for the Gairy regime."[26] But Phillip goes on to show that there were redeeming features to this performance:

> She did, however, call a Commission of Enquiry (Duffus Commission) in 1973 to investigate the breakdown of law and order in Grenada.

The Commission stated that Gairy had acted injudiciously in calling
out the police aides, known as the "Mongoose Gang", which had a
reputation for violence, to deal with the demonstrators.

Nicole Phillip also notes that "In her Christmas message in 1973,
Bynoe tried to mediate between the opposing factions and the Gairy
regime when she called for peace and unity. She called for a fresh start
and pointed out that while there would always be differing views,
Grenadians should concentrate on the common ground, the common purposes, and the common aspirations." Phillip ends her
assessment by pointing out that in her 1972 address to CARIWA, the
Governor urged women to seek "opportunity and independence
rather than concentrate solely on charity and patronage, the task to
which most middle-class women committed themselves."[27]

When Phillip assesses Dame Hilda Bynoe as a political appointee,
therefore, she perceives problems with how she performed politically in her post, that is, vis a vis the Gairy government and her
responses to that government. When she considers tasks undertaken
to ensure good government or to advance the position of women, her
tone is more positive. The low-point both for Grenada and for Dame
Hilda seems to have been related to her attempts to balance her
personal agenda with that of the Gairy regime.

I asked the Grenadian historian Caldwell Taylor what he thought
about the role of Peter Bynoe in the Grenadian story. How did he act?
How was he perceived? Caldwell Taylor commented that "most
people saw him as a fella who knew his place: his wife was the boss
and he had the good sense to walk a step behind. An architect, he
played a key role in planning of the Expo '69; and, again, he kept his
role away from the lights and that won him respect."

Dame Hilda Bynoe must be honoured and remembered for her
pioneering role as the first local governor, someone who had to write
her own book of rules. She was a woman operating in the world of
the authoritarian male Caribbean inheritors of a patriarchal British
colonial system of government. She had few precedents to guide her.
Her speeches and her life story show that she had quite radical ideas
on race, class, gender and political authority. Her 1968 elevation to
the role of governor was as sudden as her precipitate departure from
the post in 1974. But in those six years there was a major shift in
Caribbean political sensibilities and the beginnings of a struggle
between those who wanted radical decolonisation, and those who

wanted to inherit, but not change, the bequeathed tools of colonial authority. The events of 1968 were full of acclaim and companionship for a pioneering woman as she walked confidently towards the sunrise. By 1974, there was assuredly less acclaim, as the ex-Governor walked hurriedly off into what must have seemed a very depressing sunset.

In Retrospect: The Relationship with the Gairy Regime

When I interviewed Dame Hilda concerning her retrospective assessment of those years, her relationship with Eric Gairy and his regime was an area of particular concern. Dame Hilda reported, "There was never a time when we didn't have difficulties." This, she concluded, was perhaps partly because she let her opinions be known. If there was some legislation with which she felt uncomfortable, "I would write him or say to him, 'I wish you would rethink this'. She learned that her mail was routinely intercepted. It went to the Premier's house at Mt Royal before it reached Government House. When she spoke to the man who delivered the mail, he told her that he had instructions to do this. When asked at what point relationships began to deteriorate, Dame Hilda said that she "can't point to a time as the beginning of a deterioration of relations". She explained that she was not dissatisfied with the accommodation given to her, and that though at the beginning there were problems with her salary, she could make decisions about her personal staff and there was, eventually, a clothes allowance. This last is the kind of consideration males might well scoff at, but one that is important for women, not necessarily because of any greater interest in fashion, but because of the critical observations of onlookers and because of the particular wardrobe demands on a woman in such a position of authority. Dame Hilda was not unhappy in the routines of the job, although she did remember irritating details like the constant additions to lists when there were parties at Government House and more to be concerned about in the whispers she heard about repressive treatment of political opponents. The definitive change came with the November 18, 1973 beatings of the JEWEL political opposition. But the conflicts dated further back. It seems at times that as Governor she needed to use an intermediary in order to have very basic communication with Premier Gairy. One period for which she had a documentary record illustrates something of the problems inherent in the relationship.

In an April 1970 conversation with Paul Scoon, then Cabinet Secretary, Dame Hilda advised that she had tried to contact Premier Gairy several times since his return to the country but had been unable to do so. Notes and letters in her personal files indicate that she had requested that Mr Scoon advise the Premier, inter alia:

(1) that she proposed to visit Barbados from 2nd to 4th May and the Premier might wish to consider the appointment of a Deputy Governor.

(2) That she would like to know whether efforts were being made to find out the names of the Black Power leaders in Grenada with a view to holding discussions to find out their aims and objects and their way of thinking so that solutions could be found for whatever problems might exist.

(3) That she would like to know whether efforts were being made to hold discussion with graduates of the UWI or other intellectuals.

(4) That she suggested that copies of printed matter – newsletters, other printed documents – issued by UWI student bodies and lecturers should be obtained by the Government Information Service. She suggested, in particular, that the government should make itself aware of the publication *Tapia*, now available in Trinidad & Tobago.[28]

(5) That she would like to know whether efforts were being made to discover why certain members of the police force are dissatisfied and why morale in the Police Force is so low.

In this attempt at conversation, important enough to her that she kept the notations in her personal files, Dame Hilda also expressed dissatisfaction with the lack of acknowledgement by the Premier of correspondence conveyed between their two offices. She referred to a petition delivered to her by students of McDonald College one week earlier, in April 1970. She advised that she had immediately forwarded this petition to the then Acting Premier but had received no acknowledgement of the communication.[29]

Dr Bynoe's files also contain a memorandum, in draft form, to the Premier, expressing frustration with the medical situation in Grenada's sister isle, Carriacou. Dr Bynoe noted that there was no doctor in Carriacou. She expressed her frustration with this situation and expressed her wish to go to Carriacou as a doctor if no one could be found to act in that role. She wrote: "I hope you will sympathise and not object to my going. My professional obligations do not permit otherwise. My official duties can be performed from Carriacou." She added, "I hope of course that all this will not be necessary and that the Ministry will send a doctor."[30]

There is no indication from the files that any of these memos, letters, telephone communication through others, were ever answered. One letter, written when her personal secretary Ms Faye Rapier was about to leave, enquiring about her replacement and dated Wednesday 29th March 1972, reads in part:

> Dear Eric,
> Is it possible to have a short talk? Peter and I can come across to Mt Royal, or you might wish to have lunch with us, perhaps tomorrow?[31]

The letter was signed "Hilda" and on it there is the notation, "Sent by hand" and further notes: "No reply as usual. I followed up with phone calls. The usual results."

Dame Hilda recalled a disagreement with Premier Gairy about the appointment of a Supervisor of Elections. She had been given a document stating that the Premier was "advising" her to appoint Ernest John to this post. She objected, saying that the accepted wording was that she should make such an appointment in her own "deliberate judgement". She also remembered an occasion when she was unhappy with advice given her by Attorney General Armand Williams, who was "my cousin and good friend". But Mr Williams was Attorney General, and the Governor needed someone to give her advice so that she could make her own judgements. She concluded that there was a culture of fear, as those who served the state felt vulnerable and were conscious that their jobs were on the line. At one time, she noted: "practically every magistrate had been appointed on a contract basis" and they felt that they had to be careful in order to keep their jobs. These, according to Dr Bynoe, were some of the issues she considered very troubling during her tenure of office.

I asked Dame Hilda what had given her the confidence to approach the elected premier on these issues. Her response focused on both her perceived roles as governor, and her identity as Hilda Gibbs, of rural St. David's:

I saw myself, peasant daughter that I am, as a kind of bridge between the two sides. You reach Grenada, you're sworn, next morning you wake up and you're the governor. You have an office to go to. I had to understand the duties of the office, the limitations of the office. I had to understand what Associated Statehood meant. The way to do that was to read the constitution and understand it. I had nobody to understand it (for me). I soon learnt it wasn't just the constitution, that there were books of law other than the constitution. There was no advisor for the governor. There were ministers and other lawyers. There was the attorney general. It took me a while to understand that the attorney general, who, incidentally, was my cousin and good friend, Armand Williams, was not my advisor. I eventually had a legal advisor, a solicitor general, a Trinidadian brought in by the Government of Grenada. When the time came, though, I think he gave me the wrong advice. In a conversation about that document from the premier advising me to appoint Mr Ernest John as supervisor of elections, I said to him, "You are my advisor. You know that this is wrong. How can you advise me to sign this document?" He told me, 'It's all very well for you, but I could be without a job tomorrow.'

It was evident that Dame Hilda felt that there were attempts to exert undue political influence in areas where the role of the governor should, theoretically, have been above partisan political party influence. But in an Associated State, with no British queen responsible for internal affairs, where did she find the confidence to challenge the apparently authoritarian rule from an elected leader? The Chief Justice of the Associated States, she explained, was helpful here. He responded honestly when she questioned him. He advised her that the governor could make an appointment "in (her) deliberate judgment", but was not legally bound to accept the advice of the premier. This, then, gave her a certain measure of authority and did not leave her subject always to the advice of the premier. She therefore knew that the premier had no legal right to require her signature on notices stating that, "the Premier advises". There was nothing in the constitution to prevent the premier from making a suggestion to the governor that a particular person should be supervisor of elections, for example, but the premier had no constitutional right to require the governor to sign a document naming as supervisor of elections an individual chosen by him. She did things in her own "deliberate judgment" and could protest, for example, to late additions to lists of people invited to dinner at Government House. As governor, she had apparently felt that some things were in bad taste, and she said this to Premier Gairy. "As a woman," she explained to me, she wanted things to be done properly, wanted to set an example of a high moral standard, and she told the premier this. Premier Gairy advised Dame Hilda that it was for him, and not her, to give examples of morality to Grenada.

I asked her about the traditional ceremonial role of the Governor, the Queen's representative, who was not someone who had – or who expressed – political opinions. She acknowledged that, "Yes, it was the Governor's duty to have a ceremonial role, walk around in the hospitals, for example, and shake hands. I would not accept that role. I would ask questions." She paused, reflected, and said in Creole, the language she used with the characteristic ease of Caribbean people of any class: "You shaking hands and your heart breaking."

It seems that Dame Hilda always commented publicly when she thought it right to do so. When a British company discussed plans for extending electricity out of the urban areas in and around St George's, over the Grand Etang hills in the middle of the island, and on to Grenville, St Andrew's, the town generally considered second in importance to St George's, she wanted to know why not to rural St David's, on the eastern side of the island, as well? Like a politician concerned for her constituency, she could not maintain the ceremonial silence traditionally expected of the Queen's representative.

Accordingly, when Dame Hilda heard of a Cabinet decision of 31st March, 1969, to sell lands around Government House to a Mr Peter Ottley, she wrote to the Premier to ask him to "note my views on the decision". Again, there is a copy of the letter in her files:

> (1) With respect to the lands being part of the grounds which are part of the Governor's home, it would appear to me that the courtesy of prior information of your intention could have been conveyed to me.
> (2) My attitude to Government House and its grounds is that they are part of Grenada's national monuments. It is my honour and privilege to live in it and to care for it as a public servant. It is one of Grenada's institutions which we should improve upon but never destroy.

Funds for the Governor

Dame Hilda Bynoe was not as good at requesting funds for her personal use. She had not been given and had not even thought of requesting a wardrobe allowance until Derek Walcott's then wife, Margaret Walcott, mentioned that she envied her that perk of her office.

Similarly, Dame Hilda hadn't thought about securing arrangements regarding her pension. Under Grenada ordinances, she explained, parliamentarians and civil servants were accorded a pension. No provision was made for the Governor. Subsequently realising the injustice of this, Dame Hilda had raised the issue with successive administrations in Grenada. None has yet settled the matter, although in 2011 the administration indicated that the matter was under consideration.[32]

Return to Trinidad

It was the carnival season when the Bynoes decided to return to Trinidad. They had been offered a job in Guyana, but, explained Dr Bynoe, her husband's "navel string" was buried in Trinidad, and, after the recent traumatic events, he wanted to be home. Individual reactions matter. At the airport in Trinidad, a young man, a worker, conveyed to Dame Hilda the image of a supportive and approving Trinidad & Tobago. "We're glad that you are out," he told her, and added that if at any time he could do anything, he would be happy to help. This young man became symbolic to her of a sympathetic nation, and she had the impression that Trinidad was welcoming her back, although there were some who were disappointed that she had left office. Some felt she should have been more diplomatic and found a way of riding out the crisis. After what happened later, after the Grenada Revolution of 1979, when Prime Minister Gairy was ousted in a revolutionary coup, these critics, she said, had a different opinion. They thought she had been right to leave. At the time, she said, she couldn't explain the Grenada situation to those not there to see for themselves.

At first, Dame Hilda felt lost in Trinidad, unable to relax at her first public outing, a carnival fête at the Little Carib theatre. There were many questions she had to ask herself in this immediate post-Grenada period. She had to decide how to proceed with her professional life. She had left her medical practice in the care of a woman named Dr Sonia Roche, who was married to Dr Bynoe's nephew. Dr Roche had, of course, no warning that the Bynoes' departure from Grenada was imminent, so she was still in the practice. The Bynoe home in Trinidad had also been leased. At first, while they looked around for living quarters of their own, the Bynoes lived with Peter's brother, Dr

Quintin Bynoe, his wife and family. Eventually, they found an apartment "at the back of the country club", in a "nice little locale". Friends
in Trinidad were helpful with post-Grenada healing:

> There was one friend who came and she sat with me talking,
> welcoming me back, saying that… you need your friends… and
> she's looking at an empty wall and suddenly she says, 'You'll see
> me tomorrow,' and I'm wondering, well, why I should see her again
> so quickly. And tomorrow she came with a beautiful painting, which
> adorned my wall until I didn't need it any more. Ursula Brathwaite,
> was her name.

Ursula Brathwaite had been her friend before Grenada. Several
friends gave this kind of support. When it mattered, friends and
family, whether or not they shared her political perspectives, were
there to help her make her transition back into another way of life.

In Trinidad, the Bynoes had an upstairs apartment. The landlord
and landlady lived downstairs and were kind, Dr Bynoe recalled.
They did their own housekeeping, sharing the cooking and cleaning,
"like in our student days". As they went about re-energising their
separate professional careers, the Bynoes were negotiating to get their
house back.

> We gave notice to the tenants that we were not renewing… we had
> no problems with him… we got back our house and we moved in
> to (our house at) 5a Barcant Avenue, Maraval.

Dr Bynoe also decided to go to Exeter for a refresher course in
medicine – "alone, Peter did not come with me." She spent the time
at Exeter refreshing her professional knowledge and skills. In poems
published in her creative writing collection, *I Woke at Dawn*, she
refers to autumn in Exeter and the cold weather. During that post-
Grenada period, as she went through bouts of depression, as she
worked at picking up her medical practice again and allowed herself
to be healed by the welcoming words of friends and relatives, Dr
Bynoe wrote several poems and vignettes.

In England, too, she found friends anxious about her welfare. A
family named Erinson, who had resided in Grenada, sought her out
to see if there was anything they could do. "There was lots of
goodwill," she said. People were willing to help or to just let her know
that they were there and felt supportive. When Mr Erinson saw the

very basic student conditions under which the ex-governor now lived, he spoke in admiration of her survival spirit and the way she was handling her circumstances. At the time, Dr Bynoe explained, she lived in one room of a boarding house, sharing bathroom facilities. Next door to her was a student from Costa Rica who was doing postgraduate work in cosmetic surgery and, on the same floor, "two brothers from Africa" who were at secondary school. Precipitously, she had moved from pomp and ceremony to a basic type of student apartment. After the three-month refresher course, once she was back in Trinidad, Dr Bynoe considered again how to put together a medical practice.

The transition was not without its bumpy moments. From being a regional governor due all the courtesies of her post, Dame Hilda was now Dr Bynoe, resident in Maraval, Port-of-Spain. Both sides, ex-governor and the Trinidad government, had to figure out the protocol of the new and unprecedented situation. In colonial times, when governors were finished with their period of office, they moved back to England, settling back into civilian life in a large country where their previous activities were known to few of the population. Dr Bynoe's situation was different. She paid a courtesy call on the Ministry of Health, though her husband advised her against going back to work with the Civil Service, and she decided to move back into private practice.

She contacted those who had greeted her with welcoming words and who had expressed a wish to work with her. Germaine Pantalleon, who had worked with her in the past and was trained as a nurse's aid and office receptionist, had already informed Dr Bynoe that she was happy to see her back and indicated that she would be available to work if required.

Dr Bynoe set about organising an efficient practice. In addition to Ms Pantalleon, there was an older nurse and an office secretary. Dr Bynoe now had more staff than before. Some companies, for example TELCO, the present TSTT,[33] put her on their panel of doctors. Dr Bynoe was pleased, too, that patients from her pre-governor days seemed happy to have her back. Because she had walked carefully on her way up the social ladder, had been caring and thoughtful with her patients, there were friends waiting to greet her now that she had climbed down from the heights. Of this return to private practice Dr Bynoe said when we spoke: "I enjoyed it very much."

It was a thriving practice and had the reputation for being a caring one. Dr Bynoe told me that "nobody was ever turned away because they couldn't pay." There were even times when she helped her patients by giving them money to purchase the medication they couldn't afford.

She had a particular interest in psychosomatic diseases, the effects of stress on physical health. This was a continuation of her pre-Grenada interests. She had been interested in psychiatry and had been exploring possibilities in that field before the invitation to be governor of Grenada. Some post-Grenada associations, however, were different. There was no longer the connection with Social Services through the Hon. Muriel Donawa McDavidson, for example. Audrey Jeffers, on whose advice she had depended before going to Grenada, had died the very month that she started her tenure as governor. Some circumstances had changed and she had to find her way in a new environment.

As the years passed, the practice grew. Other people were taken on and Dr Bynoe was eventually doing a morning clinic and some home visits. Later, as grandchildren came into her life and other life situations intervened, there were new interests. Finally, around 1990, Dr Bynoe averred, "I got kind of tired of medicine."

The years since qualifying as a doctor and returning to the Caribbean had offered many varied experiences. From 1954 to 1967, she had worked in Grenada, Trinidad, Guyana. Those three countries had remained the axis of her Caribbean experience. From 1968 to 1974, there was the governorship in Grenada. From 1974 to 1990, there were sixteen years in private practice in Trinidad. And then, "One day," Dr Bynoe said, "I was talking with a patient, taking a history, and the patient was talking a little while, and I found myself falling asleep. And I said, Hilda, this is a warning. You're tired. You're bored. Go home." Later she told her husband that she was tired of medicine and wanted to retire. Supportive as he had always been, Peter said, "It's up to you." So, concluded Dr Bynoe, "I retired from practice." She was then sixty-nine. "It was a shock to everybody, because doctors in those days did not retire from medicine. I was one of the first to retire, give up the practice and so on."

For three months after retirement, she was "delirious with happiness. (I was) making cups of coffee to take to my husband in bed and that kind of thing, treating him like he never got treated in the past.

Dame Hilda Bynoe, in retirement c. 2011

Because I was a student when we married ..." Three months into her retirement, however, Dr Bynoe began to miss the practice. She spent more time writing poems and vignettes. In 2011, she told me, "I still am a doctor. I got what you call retirement status from the British Medical Association and the Medical Defence Union... I can see a patient and treat a patient in an emergency." She was still a member of the Trinidad & Tobago chapter of the British Medical Council, but when she gave up her practice, she gave up responsibility for patient care. As the years passed, her ability to undertake responsibility in that area progressively decreased, and eventually she gave up her residual responsibilities for medical care.

Her basic interests, formed by her early socialisation, did not change. In November 1988, she delivered the feature address at the annual dinner of The African Association of Trinidad & Tobago's celebration of African History Month.[34]

To the end, she enjoyed having visits from her family. Children visit, grandchildren are grown, her beloved husband Peter passed away in 2003, and that, she said, was "my Calvary". Her father, Thomas Joseph Gibbs, had died and was buried at Crochu, St Andrew's on 26th February, 1978, four years after she left the post as Governor of Grenada. She was able to reflect that not only had she been a valuable medical practitioner in Trinidad & Tobago, but she could take pride from the fact that her husband, Peter Bynoe, had also excelled in his profession. In November 1979, he had been given a citation "in honour of his outstanding services to the Architects' Society of Trinidad & Tobago, whose objects are to advance the profession of Architecture."

Thomas Joseph Gibbs, in the uniform of the Knighthood of the order of Saint Sylvester in which he was invested by the Pope in the early 1970s.

Endnotes

1. Interview with Gloria Payne-Banfield, November 2011.
2. Much of this paragraph is quoted from Merle Collins, "Grenada: A Political History 1950-1979", Ph. D. Thesis, LSE, 1990. This quotation is from the section entitled "Independence and After: Struggle for the Establishment of an Effective 'Legal' Alternative'", p. 491.
3. Other (British) Caribbean countries became legally independent after these four.
4. Address by Caricom Secretary-General William Demas on Monday December 31, 1973, in *The Trinidad Guardian*. 1 January, 1974.
5. *The Trinidad Guardian,* Tuesday 1 January, 1974.
6. Creole term for mimicry, pretence, joke.
7. *1973 Manifesto of the New Jewel Movement*. See Merle Collins, "Grenada: A Political History", p. 455.
8. *The Trinidad Guardian,* 7 November, 1973, p. 1. For a discussion of the Grenada events of this period, see Collins, "Grenada: A Political History". In a country of Grenada's size, 10,000 people would suggest massive dissent, since the figure represented approximately ten percent of the entire Grenadian population.
9. Premier Eric Gairy's Broadcast to the Nation, 7 November 1973.
10. Ibid.
11. *The Trinidad Guardian*, Thursday 22 November 1973.
12. Innocent Belmar was the Assistant Superintendent of the Grenada Police Force, credited with orchestrating the beating of members of the opposition, and in particular of a group of opposition New Jewel Movement leaders including Unison Whiteman, Kendrick Radix and Maurice Bishop. Belmar, then a minister in Gairy's government, was murdered in 1978.
13. That would have been her designation in an independent Grenada.
14. Letter from the Veterans' Association, St George's, Grenada, January 11, 1974.
15. *The Trinidad Guardian,* Saturday January 12, 1974, p. 1.
16. Gillian Glean Walker, "The Witness and his Testimony." <http:/

/www.cavehill.uwi.edu/BNCCde/grenada/conference/papers/walker.html>.

17. See Igarashi, *Associated Statehood in International Law,* op.cit.

18. Caldwell Taylor, "The Road to Nationhood: A Review of the Constitutional History of Grenada. Part I", *BigDrumNation*, January-April, 2007. <http://www.bigdrumnation.org/comments/nationhood.html>

19. Thomas Perronet Thompson, "The Colonization and Commerce of British India", from *The Westminster Review*, No. XXII, October, 1829, pp. 8-9. <http://books.google.com/oks?id?id=fIcfAAAAYAAJ&printsec=frontcover&dq=thomas+perronet+thompson&hl=en&ei=jVwtTpLHG6j00gHrrLDkDg&sa=X&oi=book_result&ct=book-thumbnail&resnum=4&ved=0CD8Q6wEwAw#v=onepage&q&f=falsethumbnail&resnum=4&ved=0CD8Q6wEwAw#v=onepage&q&f=false>.

20. Thompson, 1829, p. 22.

21. Interview with Ms Winifred Telesford, Supervisor of Physical Education in Grenada, 1973.

22. George Brizan, op.cit., p. 341.

23. The Grenada airport is now an international airport and in a different location. At the time of the Bynoes' departure, the airport was a small one at Pearls, St Andrew's, in the north of the island. A new airport was subsequently built at Point Salines, South St George, by the New Jewel regime of Maurice Bishop.

24. Recent reports indicate that President of the Grenada Senate, Ms Joan Purcell, raised the matter in the Grenada Parliament and was assured that it was something of which the Grenada Government was aware and that it was under consideration. See <http://www.spice grenada.com/index.php/new-today3/114-week-ending-aug-06th-2011/211-dame-hilda-to-get-payment> which reported as follows: "The Caribbean's first woman Governor in the British Commonwealth and the first native Governor of Grenada, Dame Hilda Bynoe, for the first time will receive a gratuity payment from government. This assurance was given to Parliament by Leader of Government Business in the Senate, George Prime during a sitting last week Friday. He gave the commitment after President of the Senate,

Joan Purcell announced that after giving years of service to Grenada, Dame Hilda had never received a pension from the State and hoped that one day it would be corrected. 'An opportunity to honour Dame Hilda Bynoe who is now 89 and who travelled from Trinidad to be with us at our celebration, the first female Governor in the Commonwealth; Grenada boasts such a person. I have to regretfully add that she's never received a pension or gratuity for her years of service. I hope that one day Grenada would make good on this,' said President Purcell."

25. Nicole Phillip, op. cit. p. 101
26. Phillip, ibid.
27. Ibid.
28. *Tapia* was a publication started by Trinidad intellectual Lloyd Best, Professor of Economics at the University of the West Indies between 1957 and 1976. He died in Trinidad in 2007. The Caribbean Community Secretariat (CARICOM) notes: "in the 1960s, Best co-founded the New World Group of independent thinkers who theorised and philosophised about the economic, social and political systems of their time". See <http://www.caricom.org/jsp/projects/personalities/lloyd_best.jsp?menu=projects>.
29. From the personal files of Dame Hilda Bynoe, memo of a telephone conversation with Cabinet Secretary, Mr Paul Scoon, Saturday 25 April, 1970.
30. Draft of letter to Premier Eric Gairy, undated.
31. From Dame Hilda Bynoe's personal files, letter dated Wednesday 29th March, 1972.
32. See Note 24, this chapter.
33. Telecommunications Services of Trinidad & Tobago.
34. *The Trinidad Guardian,* 27 November, 1988.

AFTERWORD

When we were concluding our interviews, I asked Dr Bynoe if there was anything further she would like to say about Grenada and her role as Governor.

She focused on details regarding the conflicts during her final moments as Governor. She remembered a "sweet drink trunk", the owner of which was generally thought to have been involved in the government's 1974 attack on demonstrating members of the public, and to have facilitated that attack by providing a truck full of sweet drink bottles. She explained, "There were these Indian people who had a sweet drink factory... I knew them well, you know. When I say I, I mean Peter knew them well... and they claimed that they were there quite accidentally. It could be, but of course Grenadians will always believe they were there on purpose." She paused, thinking about individuals caught up in the political tensions in her island country. "I don't know," she says. "They were nice people, especially the wife. They went to live in Miami afterwards." She was clearly concerned not only to say something of her own role at a period of tremendous political tension in Grenada, but also to exonerate those whom she thinks of as innocent of the charges that might still be levelled against them by some of the Grenadian demonstrators of the period.[1]

She reflected, too, on her husband's work in Grenada. "The big thing he achieved in Grenada was Expo '69. You can't take that from him. Without him, that would not have come about. He was the person, the architect, responsible for the cultural extravaganza that came to be known as Expo '69. He had served Trinidad and Grenada and so on in Montreal, when they had that exposition, the first one that we know about, in Montreal, in '67, so he had a lot of experience about what was required and contacts in Trinidad and all around..."

She talked about education, pleased to see how the University of the West Indies has thrived following those days when it was planned in the 1940s. She told me that she thought it was important, too, to consider the work of the St George's University, an American

Peter Bynoe

institution, established in True Blue, St George's during the tenure of Premier Eric Gairy. It had moved on from those days, she said, and Grenada had to ensure that it kept affiliated with the School of Arts and Sciences. Her cousin, Lord Pitt, she continued, had also realised the importance of St George's University to the local populace.

Rooted in the stories of rural Grenada and the Caribbean, brought up to value land and to enjoy the plum and sugar apple trees and the natural vegetation of Crochu, St Andrew's and environs, Dame Hilda Bynoe was passionate about the Grenada landscape. During her period of office she was passionate, too, about ways that she might help to promote Grenada, without in any way lessening her commitment to Caribbean unity. This was not something new, not something she borrowed to be a good servant of the Queen in the colony when she became Governor. The Governor's story shows that both the rural landscape and a pan-Caribbean perspective were important parts of her early shaping. Later, at Government House she looked at the land from another angle, absorbing the urban landscape.

I asked her about how she felt when she resigned. Had she thought about her father, about whether he would be disappointed? "My father," she said, "was happy to the end. I was not worried about my father. I knew he would be all right. Everybody loved Papa. Papa was not on my mind then." Later she added, "He was happy to the end; he saw me come back, re-establish myself professionally." Her father was evidently a reflective and positive-spirited man. I saw a letter she had written in 1972 to her friend, Pearl Joseph, about when her father celebrated his 89th birthday. Dame Hilda reported that at the party held in his honour he made a speech about his batting average, appropriately using a cricket metaphor, advising the youth how to avoid being bowled out, presumably by the celestial bowler.

"Later," she told me, "I was able to make arrangements for his funeral and I was with him to the end." Her father, she reflected, was not unhappy and she had no worries about him then.

She read from a letter written 16th July, 1969, after a trip to London:

Peter and I returned home on Monday and believe it or not we were greeted at breakfast on Tuesday morning by two magnificent rainbows, stretching across the harbour from the yacht basin and disappearing behind the trees to the west of Government House grounds. Can you visualise it? It was truly magnificent. There was a very fine shower of rain, starting from the hills to the east and very slowly blanketing everything down to Grand Anse and Point Salines with what looked like a fine mist. The rain finally got to us and slowly, very slowly, the rainbows faded. I often tell people that even the rains in Grenada are beautiful and that morning gave proof to this. You can see from all this how happy we are to be back.

In retirement at her home in Diego Martin, Trinidad, during the final years of her life, she remembered it all, perhaps especially how the young woman who, like her rural counterparts, "never knew St George's", had come to have, from Government House, the view that visitors had as they entered the country, a view of the sea, the yachts, the island harbour. But as she reminded me, "I had that, the sea, but I knew who I was, so I also had all that my ancestors had, a knowledge of the land."

And she looked ahead, to the young people who will help shape the future. She turned to look at her great granddaughter Anaia, grand-child of her son Roland. She said, "She was born physically, mentally, emotionally and spiritually strong. Now that she is a year old, she is even more so. My thought is for her to continue that growth into adulthood."

Dame Hilda Louisa Gibbs Bynoe passed away at her home in Diego Martin, Trinidad, on Saturday 6 April, 2013, just after 7:00 a.m. After a long and productive life, Dame Hilda died quietly, in the Caribbean she so loved.

Endnote

1. The reference is to the day of the demonstration, 21 January 1974, when Rupert Bishop was killed by the police. Just before the shooting, the police had begun pelting demonstrators, many of school age, with bottles seized from a soft drink bottle truck.

ABOUT THE AUTHOR

Merle Collins was born in Aruba to Grenadian parents who returned to Grenada soon after her birth. She had her primary and secondary education in St George's, Grenada. In 1972, she graduated from the University of the West Indies, Mona, Jamaica, with a degree in English and Spanish. She then returned to Grenada, where she taught English and Spanish. She has also taught in St Lucia. In 1980 she graduated from Georgetown University, USA, with a Masters in Latin American Studies. She was involved in the Grenadian revolution and served as a Coordinator for Research on Latin America and the Caribbean. She left Grenada in 1983. In 1990, she graduated from the London School of Economics with a Ph.D. in Government.

Her first collection of poetry, *Because the Dawn Breaks*, was published by Karia Press in 1985. At this time she was a member of African Dawn, a performance group combining poetry, mime and African music. In 1987, she published her first novel, *Angel*, which follows the lives of both Angel and the Grenadian people as they struggle for independence. This was followed by a collection of short stories, *Rain Darling*, in 1990 and a second collection of poetry, *Rotten Pomerack*, in 1992. Her second novel, *The Colour of Forgetting*, was published in 1995, and a further collection of poetry, *Lady in a Boat*, in 2003. In 2010 she published a second collection of short stories, *The Ladies Are Upstairs*, and a revised edition of *Angel* (both with Peepal Tree), where she took the opportunity to reflect further on the collapse of the PRG and the American invasion of 1983.

She currently teaches Caribbean Literature at the University of Maryland. Her critical works include "Themes and Trends in Caribbean Writing Today" in *From My Guy to Sci-Fi: Genre and Women's Writing in the Postmodern World*; "To Be Free is Very Sweet" in *Slavery and Abolition*; and "Are you a Bolshevik or a Menshevik?: Mimicry, Alienation and Confusion in the Grenada Revolution", in *Interventions*.

INDEX